An Introduction to Economic Reasoning

To Richard Martin,

Best wishes,

David G.

David Gordon

Ludwig von Mises Institute
518 West Magnolia Avenue
Auburn, Alabama 36832-4528

D1377411

Published by the Ludwig von Mises Institute, 518 West Magnolia Avenue, Auburn, Alabama 36832-4528. (www.mises.org)

ISBN No.: 0-945466-28-5

*D*edicated to
Quinten E. and Marian L. Ward,
with deepest gratitude.

Acknowledgements

I am first of all indebted to Mr. and Mrs. Quinten E. Ward, whose generous support made this book possible. Mr. Ward's career and achievements exemplify the free market in action.

For very helpful comments on the manuscript, I thank Hans Hoppe, Jeffrey Herbener, Joseph Salerno, and Mark Thornton. They bear no responsibility for any remaining mistakes.

At the Mises Institute, Judy Thommesen and Kathy White handled editorial work in the manuscript with great skill. I thank Mises Institute Member Richard Perry for preparing the index. Pat Barnett, as always, was a constant source of encouragement. She also provided me with helpful comments and corrections. The president of the Mises Institute, Lew Rockwell, not only commissioned the project: he nudged it along through gentle prodding. To all of these, many thanks.

Table of Contents

INTRODUCTION..IX

1 THE METHOD OF ECONOMICS.....................................1

2 ACTION AND PREFERENCE, PART 1..........................15

3 ACTION AND PREFERENCE, PART 2..........................35

4 DEMAND AND SUPPLY...55

5 THE LABOR THEORY OF VALUE................................83

6 PRICE CONTROLS...103

7 MINIMUM WAGES AND WAGE CONTROL..................117

8 MONEY, PART 1...131

9 MONEY, PART 2...147

10 THE GOLD STANDARD...161

CONCLUSION..175

GLOSSARY..177

RECOMMENDED READINGS...187

ABOUT THE AUTHOR..189

INDEX...191

Introduction

WHY STUDY ECONOMICS?

Why, indeed? A good short answer is that you can't get away from it. Almost everything you do involves economics. Why do people have to earn a living? Why do some people—heavyweight boxers, rock stars, and movie producers, for example—earn vastly more than bus drivers or policemen? What determines the price of a Big Mac, or, for that matter, a Mack truck? Whenever you have to deal with money or prices, you are talking about economics. To paraphrase Monsieur Jourdain, a character in a play by the seventeenth-century French writer Molière, you have been speaking economics all your life.

But granted the pervasiveness of economics questions, why study them systematically? After all, we are all governed by the law of gravity—try jumping off a cliff sometime if you don't think so—but does it follow that we have to study physics?

If people don't understand the basic laws of economics, we are headed for disaster. You don't have to understand much physics to know why it's not a good idea to jump off a cliff; but an economy that runs well depends on enough people grasping some simple truths about how the price system works.

As we'll see throughout this book, a sound economy depends on allowing people to act freely. If politicians interfere with the free market, or attempt to replace it entirely with socialism, we are in for trouble.

And some people are always tempted to do this. They think that by one or another hare-brained scheme, they can promote their own welfare. Unless you understand the key elements of economics, you may fall for some of these ideas. If people do so, the economy will suffer or collapse altogether; and we may lose our freedom as well. A little time spent learning economics will help you to avoid a great deal of trouble later.

WHY YOU WILL ENJOY ECONOMICS

Thomas Carlyle, a famous British writer of the nineteenth century, once called economics "the dismal science." But, if economics is studied in the right way, it's a lot of fun. This may surprise you, if you have ever looked at a college textbook on economics. Most textbooks have so many equations in them that they look like a railroad timetable.

We won't be doing that here. This book contains no complicated math. But at this point you have probably thought of an objection. Even if this book doesn't have complicated math, this is not enough to make studying it fun. After all, English grammar doesn't use math either, but most students don't rank it among the most enjoyable subjects in their school careers.

Franklin D. Roosevelt

Rather, the main reason economics is fun is this: You don't have to accept anything as true just because the book says so, or your teacher tells you. Everything in economics is (or should be) a matter of reason and evidence.

As you know, this is not true for many subjects you study. Suppose, for example, you read in your history textbook: "Franklin Roosevelt saved the United States from revolution by reforming capitalism." (We assume that you are not a student in a school so "progressive" that you don't study history.)

How are you to know whether the statement about Roosevelt is true? You have to accept what the text (or your teacher) tells you. Only in college courses (and sometimes not even there) will you find out why historians make the claims they do.

Sometimes this can lead to trouble. What if the textbook is wrong? For example, the claim about Roosevelt just given is completely mistaken. Roosevelt's New Deal measures were disastrous. You may end up "knowing" things that just aren't true.

Is the solution not to believe what your teachers tell you? No, (or at least not always)—then you couldn't learn history at all. There is simply so much to learn that you have to start somewhere. Only after you have learned a great deal will you be in a position to understand why historians make the statements they do.

You will encounter the same thing when you study science. Why is "the sun is millions of miles distant from the earth" true, but "the moon is made of green cheese" false? You won't be able to find out unless you accept (at least temporarily) a great many other statements just on faith. This situation can sometimes lead to frustration. You must learn things without understanding why they are true. Wouldn't it be great to study a subject in which you don't have to do this?

But haven't we already gotten into trouble? Why should you believe the claim this book made about Roosevelt? (That is, the claim that it is false that FDR saved capitalism.) Are you being asked to accept this on faith? Not at all. By the end of the book, you will understand why the economic policies that Roosevelt followed could not work.

WHAT IS ECONOMICS?

So far, there is a major gap in our chapter. We've predicted that you will like economics, because you don't have to rely on authority.

But we have neglected to tell you what economics is. Has the ostensible subject of this book been forgotten?

As you can guess, the answer is no. An explanation of method is essential to understand economics, as we propose to do here. In one sense, it's obvious what economics is about; topics such as prices, wages, production, banking, inflation, the business cycle, etc., readily come to mind. One way to proceed would be to make a list of these, and similar topics, and then tell something about each one.

This "method," if it can be called that, was actually used by some economists in the nineteenth and twentieth centuries. In Europe, these economists were called historicists; in the United States, institutionalists. As you may imagine, economics done this way is unsystematic: it isn't at all a matter of applying deductive reasoning. In historicist economics, you *do* have to take practically everything on the book's say-so. "Economists" such as Gustav Schmoller, Werner Sombart, and Thorstein Veblen, who belonged to these schools, very rarely engaged in deductive reasoning. Their attitude was "Take down what I give you or get out!"

The economics followed in this book is that of the Austrian School, founded by Carl Menger in the nineteenth century and

Gustav Schmoller
1838–1917

Werner Sombart
1863–1941

Thorstein Veblen
1857–1929

Carl Menger
1840–1921

Ludwig von Mises
1881–1973

Murray N. Rothbard
1926–1995

continued in the twentieth century preeminently by Ludwig von Mises and Murray Rothbard. Rather than take economics to be a loosely-put-together list of topics, it is characterized by a strictly deductive approach.

Austrian economists start from a single principle, the "action axiom"—all men act. From this axiom, and a few added assumptions, we will attempt to deduce significant truths about all of the topics mentioned in the previous paragraphs but one. You will be the judge of our success. But before we can see how Austrian economics proceeds, we must first explain deduction.

1. When is it reasonable to accept judgments, "just because the book says so?"

2. See whether you can find out why Carlyle called economics "the dismal science."

Chapter 1
The Method of Economics

DEDUCTIVE METHOD

In economics, we operate with deductive logic. (Bertrand Russell, a twentieth-century English philosopher, once said that there are two kinds of logic, deductive and bad.)

Deductive logic is a tool of amazing power. Given a true statement, we can, by using deduction, obtain other true statements from it. These new statements not only are true—their truth is guaranteed! If the statements we started with are true, then our conclusions are also true.

Let's look at a few examples:

- **ALL COMMUNISTS ARE TWO-HEADED MONSTERS**

- **KARL MARX WAS A COMMUNIST**

- **THEREFORE, KARL MARX WAS A TWO-HEADED MONSTER**

Does the conclusion, "Karl Marx was a two-headed monster," follow from the premises (the statements it was deduced from)? Yes, it does. Then, if the premises are true, so is the conclusion.

Have we proved that Karl Marx was a two-headed monster? Not so fast. All we know is that if the premises are true, then so is the conclusion. Unless both premises are in fact true, we can't claim that they show the conclusion to be true.

What good is logic, then? Well, let's go over the basic point again. We know that whenever the premises are true, the conclusion is true. An argument in which the conclusion is correctly deduced from the premises is called a valid argument. If we can (somehow) arrive at true premises, then we are guaranteed true conclusions. And, as you will discover in this book, sometimes obvious truths can have very startling consequences.

But this raises a further question. What are the rules for correct inference, and how do we know these rules are true? Are we back to accepting things just because the book says so? Again, not at all.

The discipline that studies the rules of valid reasoning is logic. In this book, we won't be studying these laws in a systematic way. But the rules of inference we'll be using are very simple, common-sense ones. You will be able to see right away that they are right.

Let's look at the example just presented. The first, or major, premise, can be diagrammed like this:

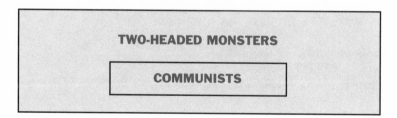

Similarly, we can diagram the second premise:

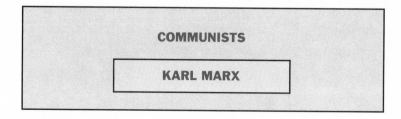

And then the conclusion:

```
┌─────────────────────────────────────────┐
│                                         │
│          TWO-HEADED MONSTERS            │
│                                         │
│     ┌─────────────────────────────┐     │
│     │         KARL MARX           │     │
│     └─────────────────────────────┘     │
│                                         │
└─────────────────────────────────────────┘
```

The inference rule we are using is: If class *a* is included in class *b*, and class *b* is included in class *c*, then class *a* is included in class *c*. You can see, just by thinking about it, that this rule is correct.

1. **How would you argue with someone who refused to accept the rule of inference given in this section?**

2. **The basic rules of logic were first discussed in detail by the Greek philosopher Aristotle (384–322 B.C.). Try to find out something about his life. Who was his teacher? Who was his most famous student?**

THE LAWS OF LOGIC

Now, we are going to dig a little deeper. Aristotle asked an important question. Why are the inference rules of logic true? He thought that there are three laws that provide a foundation for all logical truth.

These laws are sometimes called laws of thought, but this is a misnomer. According to Aristotle, these laws govern reality. The three laws are the following:

1.   A = A: The Law of Identity

2.   Not (A and not A): The Law of Non-Contradiction

3.   A or not A: The Law of Excluded Middle

We only have time to give a very brief account of these here. The Law of Identity means, as Bishop Joseph Butler put it, that "a thing is what it is." It's hard to state this in a form that doesn't repeat the principle. If you don't yet get it, some example might help: If this book is boring, then this book is boring. If roses are red, then roses are red. If roses are yellow, then roses are yellow. What would be simpler?

The Law of Non-Contradiction is equally easy to grasp. Let's use the same set of examples as before suitably modified. If this book is boring, then it is not the case that this book is not boring. If roses are red, then it is not the case that roses are not red. If roses are yellow . . . (you fill in the rest).

The hardest of the three laws for students to get is the third one. Suppose we take any two contradictory properties, e.g., red and not red (to get the contradictory of a property by negating it). Anything must be either red or not red. Thus, the number five is not red. Rudolph the Red-Nosed Reindeer's nose is red. The Gross National Product is not red. Anything whatever is either one or the other of any set of contradictory qualities.

1.   Can something be both red and not red?

2.   Some philosophers have denied that these laws are always true. Marxists say, e.g., that everything is constantly changing; therefore, the Law of Identity isn't true. Why is this objection based on a misunderstanding of the Law of Identity?

VALIDITY

We now know that if you start with true premises, you will arrive at a true conclusion. A valid argument transmits truth from the premises to the conclusion. What happens if one of the premises is false? Does this make the conclusion false? Not necessarily. All our rule says is that true premises transmit truth: it says nothing about how premises and conclusion are related with a false premise.

In the example already used, the major premise is false. It's not the case that all communists are two-headed monsters. The conclusion is also false: Marx was not a two-headed monster. But this pattern by no means always holds true. Let's look at another example:

- **ALL SCORPIONS ARE DEMOCRATS**

- **HILLARY CLINTON IS A SCORPION**

- **THEREFORE, HILLARY CLINTON IS A DEMOCRAT**

Both the premises are false. (Perhaps the falsity of the second premise is arguable!) But the conclusion is true: Hillary Clinton is a Democrat! How can this be?

By now, you should know the answer. The conclusion is true, but the premises don't make it true. These premises do not transmit truth, since they are false. Just to make things absolutely clear, all the premises must be true for truth to be transmitted. One false premise prevents the rule from applying.

Notice that the rule requires both true premises and a valid argument. This example does not meet our requirement:

- **SOME TEXANS ARE TALL**

- **SOME TALL PEOPLE ARE DEMOCRATS**

- **SOME TEXANS ARE DEMOCRATS**

This argument is invalid: the conclusion does not follow from the premises. Can you see why? Let's resort to diagrams again:

The first premise:

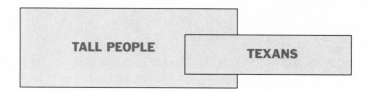

The first premise says that the classes of tall people and Texans intersect, or have some members in common. It does not say that the class of Texans is included in the class of tall people. (Can you give the premise for which this is the correct diagram?)

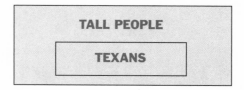

Similarly, the second premise looks like this:

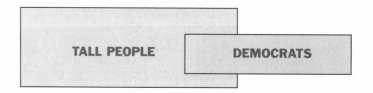

It states that *these* two classes, tall people and Democrats, intersect.

You can now see why the conclusion does not follow. The conclusion, some Texans are Democrats, looks like this:

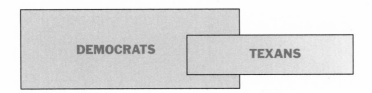

Our premises allow this to be true, but they don't require it. This is also consistent with our premises:

Both premises will be true, and the conclusion turns out to be false. Can you see how this is possible? Once again, use of a diagram will help. Suppose this was the situation:

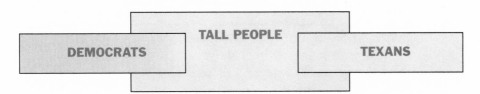

Here, both of our premises are represented. The diagram shows that some Texans are tall, and also that some tall people are Democrats. But, in this state of affairs, no Texans are Democrats. The tall people who are Texans are different tall people from those who are Democrats.

In fact, of course, both of the premises are true; and so, is the conclusion. Lyndon Baines Johnson, whom most of you won't recall, was both. (If you do remember LBJ, what are you doing still in school?) Even though premises and conclusions are both true, the premises do not transmit their truth to the conclusion, since the argument is invalid.

Can true premises in an invalid argument lead to a false conclusion? Certainly.

- **ALL AUSTRIAN ECONOMISTS SUPPORT THE SUBJECTIVE THEORY OF VALUE**

- **NO AUSTRIAN ECONOMIST LIVED BEFORE THE NINETEENTH CENTURY**

- **THEREFORE, NO SUPPORTER OF THE SUBJECTIVE THEORY OF VALUE LIVED BEFORE THE NINETEENTH CENTURY**

As we shall see later in this book, both of the premises are true, but the conclusion is false.

?

1.   Diagram the argument just given. Show why the conclusion does not follow.

2.   Give examples of (a) valid arguments with true premises; (b) valid arguments with at least one false premise; (c) invalid arguments with at least one false premise; (d) invalid arguments with true premises. Must any of these types always lead to a false conclusion?

STILL MORE ON VALIDITY

Fortunately, we have only one more rule to cover about transmission of truth. In a valid argument, if the conclusion is false, then at least one of the premises must be false. A valid argument transmits the falsity of the conclusion to at least one premise. Once again, an example:

- **MINIMUM WAGE RATES LEAD TO UNEMPLOYMENT**

- **LUDWIG VON MISES FAVORED MINIMUM WAGE RATES**

- **THEREFORE, MISES FAVORED A GOVERNMENT POLICY THAT LEADS TO UNEMPLOYMENT**

Here, the conclusion is false: *how* false you will discover later in the book. But the argument is valid. Then, our rule tells us that at least one of the premises is false. In this case, it is the second premise. Mises, who is one of this book's heroes, opposed minimum wage laws. But the first premise is true; and by the end of the book, you will be able to explain why. Thus, our rule does *not* say that in a valid argument with a false conclusion, *both* premises are false. It says that *at least one* is false. And if in fact just one premise is false, the rule doesn't tell us which one it is.

1. Show, using diagrams, that the argument about Mises is valid.

2. Give examples of a valid argument with a false conclusion that has (a) one false premise and one true premise; (b) two false premises.

3. Suppose you have an *invalid* argument with a false conclusion. What can you tell about the truth of the premises?

DEDUCTION EXTENDED

The type of argument that we have been discussing so far is called a *categorical syllogism*. It has two premises, both statements of (alleged) fact, and a conclusion. But not all valid arguments take this form: it was discussed here because you can easily grasp what validity means if you take examples of this kind. But premises can also be hypothetical. For example, the statement: "If wishes were dollars, Social Security would be financially sound" does not claim either that wishes are dollars or that Social Security is financially sound. All that the statement claims is that *if* wishes were dollars, *then* Social Security would be sound. A syllogism can have either one or two hypothetical premises.

1.   **Give examples of syllogisms with (a) one and (b) two hypothetical premises.**

2.   **Can you show how to convert a hypothetical premise into a categorical one? That is, show how an "if-then" statement can be changed into another statement about a matter of fact. If you can answer this, you will have no difficulty getting an "A" in the course. In fact, you are probably in the wrong class.**

DEDUCTION FURTHER EXTENDED

We have just a little bit more technical machinery to get through. Unfortunately, this is the most difficult section of the chapter. Fortunately, it isn't very long. Some premises are *stronger* than mere factual claims. Let's return to a variant of an old friend: "Some communists are two-headed monsters." This (false) premise does *not* say that some communists *have* to be two-headed monsters, i.e., that they couldn't possibly be anything else. It just says that they *are in fact* two-headed monsters.

Contrast this statement with the following: "No one can be his own father." This does not just say that *no one* is *in fact* his own father: it makes the stronger claim that *no one possibly could be* his own father. No matter how we change features of the actual world, this statement is always true. It's part of the *nature* of being a father that you can't be your own father.

Necessarily true propositions (but not the one about fathers) play an important part in economics, and you would be well-advised to reread the preceding paragraph carefully. (Instructors should police students at this point to make sure students understand what a necessary proposition is. If necessary, mild electric shocks may be administered.)

Now for the hard part: In a categorical syllogism, one that does not contain necessarily true premises, the conclusion need not itself be necessarily true, even though it follows of necessity from the premises. Got that? Let's have another look. Consider this case:

- **SOME ECONOMISTS ARE STUPID**
- **NO AUSTRIAN ECONOMISTS ARE STUPID**
- **THEREFORE, SOME ECONOMISTS ARE NOT AUSTRIAN**

The initial premise is (alas!) true. The truth of the second premise is a matter for discussion. But neither premise is necessary: it could have turned out, however unlikely, that all economists are intelligent. And though difficult to conceive of, it might have been the case that there are stupid Austrian economists. And the conclusion is also not necessarily true. All economists might have turned out to be Austrian economists. (Austrian economics is the foundation for this book. See page 19 for an explanation.)

Nevertheless, the conclusion necessarily follows from the premises. *If* the premises *are* true, then it *must be* the case that the conclusion is true. Given our two premises, it must be the case that some economists are not Austrians.

Then why is it wrong to say that the conclusion is necessary? If it *must be the case* that some economists are not Austrians, isn't this just what it means to say that, necessarily, some economists are not

Austrians? Yes; but, remember we are *not* asserting that it must be the case that some economists are not Austrians. We are saying that *if* the premises are true, then some economists are not Austrians.

One more complication, and then we are out of the woods (at least for now). A syllogism with two premises that are not necessarily true can turn out to have a conclusion that is necessarily true. All that we've been trying to show is that it does not have to turn out this way. Here is an example of a valid syllogism with two non-necessary premises. (The technical term for "non-necessary" is "contingent.")

- **SOME FATHERS ARE PROFESSIONAL FOOTBALL PLAYERS**

- **ALL PROFESSIONAL FOOTBALL PLAYERS ARE MALE**

- **SOME FATHERS ARE MALE**

Although the conclusion follows from two contingent premises, it itself is necessarily true. (Why? Because it follows directly from the necessarily true "All fathers are male." There is a complication here [having to do with "existential import"] that we can ignore. Some logicians don't think "All fathers are male" entails "some fathers are male." Why not? In their view, "all fathers are male" means "if x is a father, x is male." This does not entail that there are *any fathers*. But "some fathers . . ." *does* entail that there are fathers. See, I told you we should ignore this.)

We're now over the hard part. It was important to look at necessary propositions, as they play a key role in economics.

And there is one further extension we need to look at. Not all valid deductive arguments are syllogistic. Putting that into English, a valid argument doesn't have to have two premises. Suppose we start with this premise: "All socialists are subversives." From this, we may at once deduce: "All fatheaded socialists are fatheaded subversives." No intermediate premises are needed.

This sort of immediate inference is very important in economics, especially of the Austrian variety. We often are given a concept and then required to deduce various features of it that follow immediately. As we shall see, the concept of "action" is the most important one we use in economics. Much of economics consists of deducing what follows from the concept of action, and a good deal of this inference is immediate rather than syllogistic.

1.   How can you find out if a statement is necessarily true?

2.   If a statement is necessarily true, do you need to test it to find out whether it is true?

ECONOMICS VS. MATHEMATICS

But if economics proceeds strictly by logic, so that you don't have to accept statements on authority, doesn't this mean that economics is really mathematical, after all? In math, you operate through proof. Suppose $x = 5$. Then, $2x = 10$. (Don't worry, this is the toughest math in the book.) $2x = 10$ is true because it follows from applying the rule if you multiply one side of an equation by two, you must multiply the other side by two also. You arrive at the conclusion, $2x = 10$, because that is what the rule tells you to do.

Economics also uses proof, but the way it proceeds often differs from mathematical proofs. In math, to reiterate, you operate by fixed rules on certain symbols. Once you know the rule, you can fill in the blank here with almost no thought: $x = 5$, $2x =$ ____. It's an almost mechanical process. But this isn't always the case in economics.

Let's return to immediate inference. In the last section, we gave an example of a valid immediate inference. Let's look at an inference that on the surface looks similar:

- **ALL SOCIALISTS ARE SUBVERSIVES**

- **THEREFORE, ALL RUSSIAN SOCIALISTS ARE RUSSIAN SUBVERSIVES**

Here, the conclusion is false. The truth of the premise is consistent with the falsity of the conclusion. Suppose all Russian socialists are Bulgarian subversives, but not Russian subversives, i.e., they want to overthrow the Bulgarian government, rather than their own. If so, the premise might be true, but the conclusion would be false.

But how do we know this? No mechanical rule will tell us which immediate inferences work, and which do not. We simply have to use our judgment; and this is often true for non-immediate inference as well.

?

1.   **How do we know the rules of mathematics are correct?**

2.   **Would it be a good idea to use symbolic logic in economics, if economics relies on immediate inferences?**

3.   **Is it always best to begin by "defining your terms"? Why or why not?**

4.   **Deduction only tells us what we already "know." How might a supporter of the deductive approach reply?**

Action and Preference
Part 1

Chapter 2
Action and Preference
Part I

After getting through Chapter 1, you may have wondered: what does all of this have to do with economics? In this chapter, we'll find out. What we are going to attempt is to apply the deductive method in order to build up a science of economics. Remember, if we carry out this task correctly, we will have achieved something remarkable. Given a true starting point, our conclusions must be true.

This at once raises a key issue. What should be chosen as the starting point? To pick the wrong initial premise threatens disaster. Suppose, for example, we started with this premise: "The economic value of a good consists of the labor necessary to make it." This statement, as we'll soon discover, is false. Anything we deduce from it, then, is not guaranteed to be true. Our conclusions may be true, but they won't be true because they follow from our starting point.

It's easy to think of true propositions that we might start with—that isn't the problem. "2 + 2 = 4" is, unarguably, true; so is "Some U.S. presidents have been big spenders." The hard part is to arrive at a true proposition that will lead to significant results. Fortunately, through the genius of the Austrian economist Ludwig von Mises, this problem has been solved.

THE ACTION AXIOM

The fundamental principle of economics can be stated in two words: man acts. Most of the rest of this book will endeavor to clarify what this axiom means, and to draw out its implications. Our first question is obvious: what is an act? Incidentally, "man" in the axiom of course refers to both men and women. "Man" is a general term that means "human beings." This is perfectly acceptable English usage, in spite of the absurd posturing of the "politically correct." Feel perfectly free to substitute "human beings" for "man" in the axiom, if you are so inclined; I can't help it if you cave in before a silly political fashion.

But I digress. What is an action? It is easier to give examples than to offer a watertight definition. Reading a book, voting for class president, doing your homework, and playing soccer are all actions. (If you have the misfortune to attend a progressive school, look up "homework" in the dictionary.) Any conscious behavior counts as action—an action is anything that you do on purpose.

> 1. "The action axiom is trivial. Everybody knows it's true. It's like 'a red light means stop'; nothing interesting follows from it." What's wrong with this argument?
>
> 2. List some other basic terms besides "action" that are hard to define exactly, even though everybody knows what they mean.
>
> 3. "Unless we define our terms, we can't think accurately. It isn't enough, then, to have an approximate idea of what 'action' means. We need an exact definition." Is this line of thought correct? Why or why not? Use your answer to the preceding question to help you with this one.

ACTION

It's important to note a basic distinction here. Not everything that happens to a person counts as an action: an action must be done deliberately. While you are reading this, your pulse is beating

(I hope). But this is not something that you have decided to do: it is a process that goes on automatically in your body. Reading, of course, is an action. You don't read just by having a newspaper page put in front of you; you have to decide to do it; and, while you're reading, the process is under your conscious control.

Some actions don't require much conscious control. For most people, walking takes place without having to think explicitly about each step. You don't say to yourself, "Left foot, right foot; now left again, etc.," you just walk. Nevertheless, the process is under your conscious control. Imagine what it would be like if things were different. Suppose you suddenly found your legs moving by themselves, and your efforts to will them to stop failed. Then you wouldn't be acting, although your body would be moving.

1.   **Are nervous tics actions? Sleepwalking? Epileptic fits?**

2.   **"Walking isn't really an action. Walking just consists of other actions, such as moving your legs." What's wrong with this argument?**

Normally, an action includes some physical movements of the body. When you walk, your legs move; when you read, your eyes are constantly shifting focus. Some "actions" don't seem to involve physical movement, e.g., thinking. (There are all sorts of things going on in your brain when you think, but are these thinking itself? Could thinking take place altogether apart from any physical entity? Fortunately, we don't have to solve these issues here.)

But the actions we'll be concerned with in economics do, for the most part, involve physical movements; examples include buying, selling, investing, and laboring. We'll take thinking for our purposes as part of action, rather than as a separate act itself. (Note, however, that ordinary usage includes "acts of thought.")

Not all outward actions, however, do involve physical movement. Suppose you are thinking about going for a walk. You decide not to; you find appealing the remark of R.M. Hutchins: "Whenever I feel like exercise, I lie down until the feeling goes away." You still act; in this context, staying put is an action.

There are even a few cases in which you can do something besides waiting or staying put without any physical movement taking place. Imagine that you are a member of Congress. A resolution has been proposed to increase taxes by 50 percent. The Speaker announces: "All those in favor, please stand; opposed, remain seated." Since you have, by the time of your election, finished studying this book, you understand why taxation is theft. You decide to vote "no"; and, following the Speaker's instructions, you remain seated. You haven't moved; but you have voted, just as much as if, ignorant of sound economics, you had stood up. To reiterate, though, most of the actions that we'll be studying do involve physical movement.

IS THE AXIOM TRUE?

Well, we have our initial axiom; and the next step appears obvious. As promised, we must deduce conclusions about economics from it. But something has been left out. Recall, we must have a true initial premise in order to be sure that the conclusions we draw from it are true. So far, all that I have done is to state the axiom, and say a few things about it. But is it true? Unless it is, we're in trouble, for the reason already stated.

Fortunately, the problem is easily solved. Isn't it obvious that the axiom is true? When I explained the axiom, I deliberately picked examples such as walking and reading that we all do. You wouldn't be reading these words now, unless you were acting. Once you think about "man acts" you will see that it is silly to doubt it. (If you think about the axiom but don't see that it's obviously true, you would be probably better off to drop economics and take up sociology instead.)

The action axiom, then, is a commonsense truth. And this is enough to get the science of economics going. In this respect, economics differs from chemistry, biology, and (most of) physics. In these sciences, we usually need to experiment in order to find things out. It isn't an obvious, commonsense truth that a molecule of water is composed of two hydrogen atoms and one oxygen atom. This was something scientists discovered only by careful testing.

Not everything in the physical sciences rests on experiment. The ancient Greeks identified a body in the sky which they called "Hesperus," the Morning Star. They picked out another body, "Phosphorus," the Evening Star. Careful observation showed that the two bodies are identical. "The Morning Star is the Evening Star" is part of astronomy, but it didn't require experiment to establish. Nevertheless, it isn't a commonsense truth: careful observation was needed to discover it.

In the physical sciences, you can sometimes get the wrong results if you rely on common sense. What could be more obvious, for example, than the fact that the sun moves round the earth. "Of course the Earth is stationary. Use your eyes!" a character in one of George Bernard Shaw's plays remarks. But in fact (or so at least modern astronomers tell us) the earth is moving at an enormous rate of speed. Common sense does not inform us of this, and common-sense observations don't refute it. "If the earth were moving, we'd all fall off" is not a good reason to doubt that the earth moves.

This suggests a problem. If, in the physical sciences, common-sense observations can turn out to be false, why not in economics as well? Perhaps the action axiom, however apparent its truth, will one day be shown false. Have we started down a false trail?

You will be glad to know that we haven't. Why do common-sense judgments about the physical world sometimes turn out to be mistaken? This involves difficult issues in the philosophy of science;

but, basically, the answer is straightforward. In the physical world, there is an underlying level of things not directly open to observation. Common sense can tell you how the world is on the surface: it does not disclose the world's inner structure.

But human action isn't like that. There is no underlying level for human action, in the same way that there is for the physical world: What you see is what you get. Since we act ourselves, we grasp the nature of action directly. We don't have to guess at the inner structure of thought. Physical objects consist of atoms, but there aren't "atoms of thought."

1.   "Yes, there are too 'atoms of thought'! The brain has an inner structure, just like any other physical object. And the mind is the brain. Therefore, there are atoms of thought." Evaluate this objection. (If you can show what's wrong with it, you're a ringer.)

2.   Look up Newton's first law of motion. How does this contradict common sense?

You might think that economists would be glad to have a commonsense foundation for their discipline. But some of them are not. In contrast to the Austrian School, which fully accepts the deductive approach, many economists think that it is unscientific to rely purely on deduction. Deduction plays an important role in economics, no doubt; but premises ought not to be accepted just because they are held "self-evident." Rather, what is important is the conclusions which these premises imply. These must be subject to test. Whether the premises are self-evident or even true matters little; only predictions count. As we shall see, Austrians reject this view.

A basic principle of economics, one we'll be studying soon, is the law of demand. Instead of showing how this law follows deductively from commonsense principles, some economists have conducted surveys to find out whether the law holds. They ignore the fact that, if the law has been correctly deduced, it rests on a much firmer basis than conjectures derived from polls.

MORE ABOUT ACTION

Now that we know the action axiom is true, we can return to the main business of deducing theorems from it. There isn't anything difficult or unusual in doing this: using a commonsense point of view, we shall look at the concept of action and see what we get.

For one thing, every action has a goal or purpose. Why, for example, are you now reading this page? Because you want to find out what we're attempting to communicate. (Why you want to do that is of course another question.) Again, when you walk across the classroom, you do so in order to arrive at your destination: you want to go from Point A to Point B. (Back in the Dark Ages when I went to school, I would have used the example of walking to school: but of course no one would do so odd a thing today.)

And what in turn follows from your having a goal? Obviously, you haven't already obtained the goal: otherwise, there would be no need to act. If you were already at Point B, there would be no need to move there. (Indeed, you couldn't move there. You might stay there, but that would be a different action.)

But a goal by itself does not suffice for an action. Let us return to the case of moving from Point A to Point B. It is such a thrilling example that one can hardly do otherwise. Suppose you are now at Point A. You would like to be at Point B, but you have no idea how to get there. ("It's all the way across the room! What am I supposed to do?") You so far haven't done anything. In order to act, you must do something to get what you want. You must, in other words, use means to achieve your goal. In this case, of course, walking across the room is the means to obtain your goal of being at Point B.

> 1.   **Give a few examples of acts that you have done. Identify the ends and means in each.**
>
> 2.   **Here is a difficult problem we won't be able to cover in this book that you might like to try your hand at: In order to obtain an end, you have to use means. But using means to achieve an end is itself an action. In walking across the room, e.g., I move my legs in a certain way. But, if using the means is an action, doesn't that action require the use of a further means? If so, doesn't an infinite regress result? How, then, can action take place at all? (If you find this question unintelligible, feel perfectly free to ignore it. Better yet, ask your teacher if he can answer it.)**

We now understand the basic structure of an action: the use of means to obtain an end. In turn, the question arises, what can we deduce from this? (You can begin to see how economics develops: from what we already know, we attempt to deduce more and more.) What must be true if there are ends and means?

Suppose you thought that, regardless of anything you did or didn't do now, you would wind up at Point B. Then, it would be pointless for you to start walking. Why walk if you are going to get there anyway? (Assume that walking won't get you there faster than doing nothing.) Or, suppose you thought your legs would start moving automatically. There would again be no point to setting yourself deliberately to move them. In order to act, then, you must believe that obtaining the goal is, at least in part, up to you.

Sometimes this point is put in this way: it is a condition of action that the future is uncertain. But this can be misleading. It may just mean exactly what was said before; in order to act, you can't believe that your goal will come about regardless of what you do. If so, of course, fine.

But "the future is uncertain" may suggest something else. Perhaps what is intended is that in order to act, you must not know what is going to happen. (I think, in fact, that this is the more natural reading of "the future is uncertain.")

But this is a much stronger claim, and we have not at all proved that this is a necessary condition of action. Can you see why it's a stronger claim? Well, the first claim, the one that we have argued for, is that in order to act, you must not know that the goal will come about, regardless of what you do. The new claim is that in order to act, you must not know that the goal will come about. The "regardless of what you do" clause has been dropped. And so far, at any rate, no justification has been offered for doing so.

In fact, the stronger claim is false. Sometimes (though not always) we do know our goal will come about; and our knowing this is consistent with our acting to obtain the goal. How is this possible? Suppose you know that if you walk across the room, you will arrive at Point B. You also know that you are going to walk across the room. Then, why can't it be true that you know now that you are going to be at Point B? If you do know this, then in this respect the future is not uncertain. Don't say in response that there must be something wrong with the argument, because the future is uncertain. This is just the issue in dispute.

This may sound like much ado over a very small point. (Perhaps it sounds like this because it is much ado about a small point.) But we have emphasized it because the very idea of the future makes many economists go into a panic. They think that because human action is oriented toward the future, it is what they call "radically uncertain." Actors, in their view, know next to nothing at all about what the results of their actions will be. As you can imagine, economists with this view are rather limited in what they can say: there isn't much room for a science of economics if one's only message is that actors are ignorant. It is important, then, not to fall for the "radical uncertainty" line.

?

1.   List something about the future that you know.

2.   "We don't really know the future. Suppose I think I know that I'll have ice cream for breakfast tomorrow. I always have ice cream for breakfast, and I'm a creature of habit, so my claim to knowledge appears well-grounded. But it is false. After all, I might change my mind; or I might die during the night, or untold other things might happen. Thus, I don't really know that I'll have ice cream tomorrow; and the future is indeed radically uncertain." Evaluate.

Enough about "radical uncertainty." Let's return to the structure of action. We have just learned that in order to act, you must not believe that your goal will be achieved, regardless of what you do. Can you think of a closely related belief that, if you had it, would prevent you from acting? You must not believe that your goal will fail to be achieved, regardless of what you do. Suppose we would like to be the next King of England. The job pays well, and it's fun having people bow to you. I believe, however, that nothing that I can do can in any way secure my goal: I'm just not eligible to be king, absent an unimaginable change in the Law of Succession to the Crown. My goal will thus lead to no action.

PREFERENCE AND UTILITY

An action, then, uses means to achieve an end. What follows from the fact that you are pursuing a certain end? Obviously, you want that end: you prefer having it to having something else. We return once again to our never-failing source of excitement—the move across the classroom from Point A to Point B. If you move from A to B, would you rather stay at A or be at B? Even a graduate of a progressive elementary school should be able to cope with this one. You would rather be located at B; otherwise, you wouldn't move there. Another way of putting the point is that when you act, you think you'll be better off after you obtain your goal than you would have been without it.

Economists like technical terms; so instead of saying that when you act, you think that you will be better off, they usually say that you think your utility or welfare will increase by acting. It is crucial for your understanding economics to realize that this is just a restatement of the previous point; we haven't added anything new by the claim that in acting, you think your level of utility will increase. All you have said (to go over the point once more) is that you prefer getting your goal to not getting it.

Why are we pounding you over the head with this? Because there is a mistake that is very easy to make here. Some people think that whenever you act, you are trying to maximize pleasure and minimize pain. What does this mean? There are some feelings or sensations that people tend to like; imagine how you would feel, for example, if you were right now eating a banana split instead of studying the concept of utility. Or imagine how you would feel if you saw the person you most hate in the world carried away in a flying saucer.

Other feelings of course, most people try to avoid. Very few people seek out red-hot stoves to touch; and not many would emulate King Enrique el Impotente of Castile, the father of Queen Isabella, in seeking out the smell of burning leather.

According to psychological hedonists or egoists, who hold the view about action just described, maximizing pleasure and minimizing pain are our only real goals. All actions, on this view, are means (ultimately) to increase pleasurable sensations or decrease painful ones. If we move from Point A to Point B (surprise!), we do so because we think being at Point B will better serve our happiness.

There are other forms of hedonism that view the goal of action in somewhat different ways, but this form ("crude" or "hardline" psychological hedonism) is sufficient for our purposes.

UTILITY AND WELFARE

Having explained what psychological hedonism is, we are now ready to deal with the mistake about utility and welfare to which I earlier referred. When we say in economics that an actor thinks that obtaining his goal will increase his utility, we are not—repeat not—committing ourselves to psychological hedonism. By this point you should be able to explain what an increase in utility means in economics. All that we are saying, as economists, is that an actor prefers securing his goal to not obtaining it. "Utility" and "welfare" do not designate particular ends, such as sensations of various kinds, to which our ordinary goals are means.

It is a fallacy to take welfare and utility as if they did designate particular sensations. Economists who do so think of utility as a substance that we always attempt to increase. We are, on this view, always saying to ourselves, "More utility!"

Jeremy Bentham
1748–1832

John Stuart Mill
1806–1873

But why is the position a fallacy? I believe that psychological hedonism is mistaken, but I certainly have not shown that it is. The problem with the theory, for our purposes, does not lie in its (alleged) falsity. Rather, it does not follow from the concept of action. It is a psychological hypothesis about how people act. It has no place in the deductive science of economics we are attempting to construct.

1. **Does psychological hedonism strike you as a plausible theory? How would you explain actions that aim to help other people, using this theory?**

2. **Does maximizing pleasure always lead to the same actions as minimizing pain?**

3. **Some philosophers, e.g., Jeremy Bentham and John Stuart Mill, adopted utilitarianism as an ethical theory. They held that one should try to maximize the happiness of as many people as possible ("The greatest happiness of the greatest number"). Do you think that utilitarianism is a true theory of ethics?**

Once more we return to the concept of action. Each of us, in acting, aims to achieve a goal by the use of means. We must decide what means will best secure our ends. How can I get to Point B? Should I walk? run? drive? Questions about choice of means constantly confront us.

And choice is not confined to questions of means. The Danish philosopher Søren Kierkegaard said that purity of heart is to will one thing. Perhaps he is right; but in fact people have many different ends at which they aim. We must choose not only between various means to achieve a goal, but also among goals. Will you spend the next hour studying economics? Eating ice cream? (If I were you, I would pick the latter.)

One further complication. We not only choose between goals, and choose which means to use to obtain a given goal. Many means can be used to help achieve more than one end; we must decide which end each versatile means will serve. This economics textbook might be put to use as a doorstop: is this a good use of it, given your ends? Suppose that the textbook would make a better doorstop than the bust of your great-aunt that now reposes useless in your attic. You may decide to put your great-aunt's head to use at the door, even though it is inferior to the textbook as a doorstop, if you wish to use the textbook for some other purpose.

Action, then, involves complex choices among both goals and means. I hope that you have noticed something about this proposition that differs from the points about action we have previously made. It doesn't follow from the action axiom. Do you see why not? It is perfectly consistent with the axiom that each person engage in only one action, with a fixed set of means. (Remember the legend of Sisyphus, who spent his life pushing a rock up a mountain?)

Stop! Hasn't something gone wrong? We are supposed to be developing a deductive science of economics, but we have introduced propositions that don't follow from the axiom. What is to be done? Must we give up economics as a deductive discipline?

Not at all. Economics is still deductive; but we must introduce a few extra principles besides the action axiom. Once we admit these, we can then proceed in the same deductive fashion as we have so far done. Only now we have more premises to work with.

The extra principles that we now need are these: (1) People have a variety of goals; and (2) There are a variety of resources or means by which people can pursue these goals. But how do we know these principles are true? You will recall (and if you don't your teacher will remind you) the big problem we discussed at the start of this chapter. If we don't start with true principles, then we have no guarantee of the truth of what is deduced from them. How, then, do we know that our extra principles are true?

Some Austrian economists would contend that I have taken a wrong turn in the last few paragraphs. We could understand the action axiom in a broader sense. "Action," in this extended sense, necessarily involves a variety of goals. Simple repetitive "action," it might be argued, isn't really action. To act, you must decide how to allocate a means between competing ends.

If this view is right, then the "extra principles" are really part of the action axiom. But, I'm not sure that this view is right. What do you think?

In exactly the same way that we know the action axiom is true, we know the extra principles are true. They are obviously true, commonsense propositions. It is not a conjecture, to be confirmed by careful experiment, that there are a variety of resources. It's something of which we are certain.

> **1.** **The action axiom is a necessary truth. Are the extra principles necessary truths? (You might find it helpful to look again at Chapter One.)**

We have different goals. How do we choose between them? Should I now move from Point A to Point B, eat a gallon of ice cream, or toss this book out the window, assuming that I would like to do all three? The time available, we assume, allows me to do only one.

The answer, I'm afraid, sounds trivially obvious. You rank the goals: which, of the three, would you most like to obtain? (Guess which one I would pick!) Having done so, you act to achieve your most highly-valued goal.

As usual, we have to avoid a false step. We are not saying this: you measure the goals on a numerical scale of satisfaction, and then pick the one that scores highest. Eating ice cream gives ten units of satisfaction, while tossing the book out the window rates only a three. (Moving to Point B is only slightly above the vanishing point.) This approach, measuring the goals on a scale of satisfaction, and picking the top scorer, is our old friend psychological hedonism. This is a speculative theory whose truth we do not assume in Austrian economics.

But if we rule out measurement on a scale, how can we rank our goals? Easy: we do it as follows: first goal, second goal, . . . etc. We use an ordinal, rather than a cardinal ranking. Compare the following: Mount Everest is taller than Mont Blanc, which is taller than the Hollywood Hills (ordinal ranking). Mount Everest stands x feet tall. Mont Blanc stands y feet tall (cardinal ranking). This should make the distinction clear.

In this connection, the British economist Lord Lionel Robbins compared utility to love. You can usually tell whether you love one person more than another, but you can't measure "how much" in definable units.

Now, we know what kind of ranking we are looking for. But what determines how the goals rank? Which goal ranks first? The answer may prove a disappointment to those in search of complicated theory: the actor himself decides which goal he ranks highest. He is the one who acts, after all; what counts in the explanation of what he

Lionel Robbins
1898–1984

does is his personal rank order of goals. In economics, preferences are subjective.

---

1.   Some people believe that there are objective values in ethics. What does this mean? Is this view consistent with our statement that in economics, preferences are subjective?

2.   "You haven't refuted the theory that goals are ranked cardinally on a scale of satisfaction. For all you have shown, goals are ranked this way." Evaluate. (In this connection, reread the discussion of psychological hedonism.)

I'm afraid we must now face another problem. We have said that an actor always chooses his most highly valued goal. But how do we know this is true? Suppose someone says, "My second highest goal is good enough for me; I'll do that first." Is this incoherent? Is our claim that an actor always acts to secure his most highly valued goal another extra principle, adopted because it is convenient and defended as obvious? Or can it be deduced from the principles we have already acknowledged? This question we shall address in the next chapter, where the discussion of action and preference continues.

Action and Preference
Part 2

Chapter 3

Action and Preference
Part 2

THE HIGHEST VALUED GOAL

As you will recall, the last chapter ended with a question. How do we know an actor always acts to secure his most highly valued goal? Remember, in economics our aim (our most highly valued goal) is to deduce important results from the action axiom. (What is the action axiom? Of course you know, but go back to the previous chapter and read the section on the axiom again.) Does it follow from the action axiom that an actor always will act to secure his most highly valued goal?

It's quite easy to see the answer is yes. Suppose you have a choice between watching a wrestling match between Hulk Hogan and The Undertaker, on the one hand, and listening to Hillary Clinton explain what's good for us on the other. You would rather watch the wrestling match. What should you do?

Obviously, you should watch the wrestling match. It wouldn't make sense for you to choose to listen to Hillary, given that you would rather have the alternative. (Remember, we're not concerned in economics with what you should choose. Our problem is: given your preference scale, how will you act?)

1. The principle that you always act to secure your most highly valued goal is not obviously true. In fact, it is false. I'd rather stay healthy for the next ten years than go to the

movies. But I may choose going to the movies over doing pushups or other things that I believe will make me healthier. Why is this a poor objection to the principle?

2.   Don't people often choose not to seek their highest valued goals? Suppose you can get an easy "A" on your next math test by copying the exam written by Norman Nerd, the student sitting next to you. (Norman always gets 100 percent on math tests.) You won't be caught because your teacher is nearsighted. You of course resist temptation, even though you want an "A." (If you get one, you will receive $1,000 from your parents.) Aren't you here refusing to go after your most highly valued goal?

THE TAUTOLOGY OBJECTION

We hope you spotted what was wrong with the last objection. If you think it is wrong to cheat on math exams (economics exams are of course another issue), then you prefer not cheating to cheating. If this preference outranks your desire to get an "A" on the test, then by not copying from Norman's paper, you are getting your highest preference. True enough, you may not get an "A" if you don't cheat; but this is not relevant. Of course you want an "A," but you want to be a non-cheater even more. Hence you don't cheat.

Some writers who oppose Austrian economics use this answer to help launch another objection. "If you say that you must prefer not cheating, since you chose not to cheat," they claim, "then all you are doing is defining your highest preference as what you in fact choose. You aren't saying anything new."

We may put this objection a little more formally this way:

If (1) highest preference = what you choose

then (2) you always choose your highest preference since (3) you always choose what you choose

To prove (2), all you have to do is substitute "what you choose" for "your highest preference" as (1) says you can. You then arrive at the identity (3). But this is trivial: it tells us nothing.

This objection says that a key Austrian claim is trivial. And the objection can be extended. Parallel arguments can be used to claim that other key Austrian principles tell us nothing new. It is thus far from trivial that we refute this objection.

1.   **Construct a parallel argument with the one given above that claims the action axiom is trivial. (If you need help, see the discussion of the action axiom in the preceding chapter.)**

2.   **Construct a parallel argument for the triviality of any other of the principles we have so far discussed.**

3.   **Are there any results we have so far arrived at that are not vulnerable to this objection?**

THE TAUTOLOGY OBJECTION ANSWERED

Essentially, any argument can be countered in two ways: we can find something wrong with the argument, or claim that the argument's conclusion does not matter. The philosopher Morris Cohen summed this up in a memorable way. In reply to a student, he said: "In the first place you're wrong; and, in the second place, even if you were right, so what?"

Both sorts of reply can be used against the tautology objection. First, the objection just isn't right. We did not define "your highest preference" as "what you in fact choose." Rather, we claimed something importantly true about what you choose—namely you will select your highest ranking preference.

But if we didn't define highest preference in this way, how do we know the principle is true? Well, the answer is so simple it is hard to explain in other terms: we just study the principle and see that it must be true. Why would you choose something other than your highest preference?

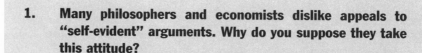

1.   Many philosophers and economists dislike appeals to "self-evident" arguments. Why do you suppose they take this attitude?

THE TAUTOLOGY OBJECTION CONSIDERED FURTHER

But suppose the objection is right. Then, our principle, "you always act to get your most highly-valued goal" is trivial, a tautology. So what? Why is this a consideration against it? (Remember that a tautology is a statement, e.g., a definition, that is true just by the meaning of the words in it.)

"What do you mean, so what? A tautology is just playing with words! If our principle is trivial, is this not an extremely damaging point against it?" This response confuses two senses of the term "trivial." In the first, the term designates what is unimportant. If our principle, or other principles of Austrian economics, is trivial in this way, that is indeed a damaging criticism. But, taken this way, the objection fails. As we'll see in the rest of the book, the principle is not useless: it is crucial for the development of economics.

In the other sense of "trivial," the word is just a synonym for "tautology." We have argued that the principle is not a tautology; but suppose that it is one. Then, it would be "trivial" in this second sense. But it does not follow that it is trivial in the first sense.

Some tautologies are important; others are not. Many philosophers think that mathematics consists of tautologies. It hardly follows, if they are right, that mathematics consists of trivialities. The subject would be much easier if it did.

1. **Give examples of tautologies that are trivial in the first sense.**

2. **What determines whether a tautology is trivial in this sense?**

MARGINAL UTILITY

Exactly how untrivial our principle is, we shall now see. Suppose you have five different goals, which you rank in this order: (1) drinking a glass of orange juice; (2) eating the whole orange; (3) stomping an orange into the ground; (4) eating an orange peel; (5) collecting all the pips in an orange to add to your orange pip collection. (Remember you rank these goals ordinally; you are not measuring them using a common unit. Also, we assume that one complete orange is required to satisfy each of these goals.)

Further, suppose you have only one orange. What will you do with it? The answer will be apparent to anyone except a hermeneutician. You will use the orange for orange juice, since this is your most highly-valued use.

Now, what if you have two oranges? Just as obviously, you will use the oranges for your first two most highly valued uses. The more oranges you have, the lower you can go on your preference scale.

Let's look at the same phenomenon from another angle. Suppose you have five oranges, which you intend to use for the five goals specified above. The oranges are equal in quality and serviceability. Now, disaster strikes. Johnny Orangeseed steals one of your oranges, leaving you with only four. What do you do, as far as the use of the oranges is concerned?

The answer is once again apparent. Your pip collection will have to do without the addition you hoped to contribute to it. Since adding to the collection is your least valued use, you will give it up first. Note that this is true regardless of which orange Johnny steals. Suppose, e.g., that he takes the orange you had planned to squash into the ground. You will then shift the orange from the pip collection to be stomped. Regardless of which orange is taken away, you will give up your least valued use. The unit of the good (in this case, oranges) that is devoted to the use you value least is called the marginal unit. As we shall see in the next chapter, this concept plays a crucial role in the explanation of prices.

1.   Show that the explanation just given of what you would do if you lost one orange follows from the principle that you always select your highest valued preference.

2.   The analysis just given doesn't work. It wrongly assumes that you have a list of preferences in your head before you choose. But in fact your preferences exist only at the moment of choice. Is this objection right?

THE INDIFFERENCE OBJECTION

You might object to our analysis in this way. We assumed that you could rank all five uses of an orange in order from first to fifth. But what if you can't? Suppose, for example, that you cannot make up your mind between eating an orange and stomping it into the ground. You are indifferent between these two alternatives. Then what will you do with your second orange if you have two of them? Your preference scale does not dictate a choice.

Let's examine the situation more closely. You have one orange, out of which you have made orange juice. (This is your highest valued use.) You now acquire a second orange but cannot make up your mind between your second and third choices.

Should you simply go on to choice four, or, overcome with indecision, toss away the new orange? Certainly not. You would rather either eat the orange or stomp it than eat the orange peel (alternative four). As to tossing the orange away, then you would not realize any of your preferences. This would be an especially foolish thing to do.

The comments just given rest on a brilliant analysis of the problem of "Buridan's ass," given by Murray Rothbard. Buridan, a great scholastic logician, imagined a perfectly rational donkey. The donkey never acts unless there is sufficient reason to do so. He has a choice of eating one of two bales of hay, identical in all relevant properties. Buridan imagined that the donkey, unable to find a reason to choose between the two bales, would do nothing and thus starve.

Rothbard pointed out that Buridan's account of the situation was incomplete. The alternatives facing the donkey are not just (1) eat bale of hay A, and (2) eat bale B. They include also (3) do not eat either bale and starve. Since, presumably, the donkey ranks (3) below either (1) or (2), he will not, as Buridan has it, choose (3). To do so would involve a violation of our fundamental principle: an actor always prefers a higher ranking goal to a lower ranking one.

1. Look up the section on Buridan in Rothbard's *Economic Thought Before Adam Smith* (Cheltenham, U.K.: Edward Elgar, 1995), and give a brief report on his work.

2. How might a supporter of Buridan's argument reply to Rothbard?

MORE ON INDIFFERENCE

A chooser, then, faced with two alternatives that seem to him "about the same" must somehow make up his mind between them. He will, e.g., flip a coin to determine whether to eat the orange or squash it. And once he has chosen, his choice counts as a preference as much as an act based on the most ardent conceivable desire. You cannot demonstrate indifference in action: given two alternatives, you must pick one or the other.

And of course it is action that we are concerned to analyze in economics. Indifference, then, plays no part in our discipline. But, you will object, what if, as in our example, you do not have a marked preference for either alternative? (Before continuing, see whether you can answer this objection.)

The key to the problem, once more, brings in a point from the previous chapter. Remember, the scale of preference is an ordinal scale: we rank alternatives only as first, second, third, . . . etc. We do not take the alternatives as containing more or less of some common unit. More generally, all we are concerned with is the fact of preference: the strength of the preference does not for our purposes matter. Thus, a preference established by flipping a coin is still a preference. The psychological state in which you decide is irrelevant for us as economists.

Here is another way of looking at the issue which may make the point at issue easier to grasp. Once more return to the oranges and the actor who, as we have learned not to say, is "indifferent" between eating an orange and stomping on it. (Since the point is so important, and since this is my book, allow me one repetition. We are not saying there is no such thing as indifference: we are saying that indifference cannot be demonstrated in action and so is not used in economics.)

Because we do not use the concept of indifference in Austrian economics, we get a bonus. Mainstream neoclassical economics relies heavily on indifference curves, Edgeworth boxes, and other complicated mathematical constructions that we do not have to bother with. Austrian economics is in this way much easier to learn than this rival system.

1. **You can *too* demonstrate indifference in action! Flipping a coin to decide between two alternatives is just a demonstration of indifference in action. Evaluate this objection.**

EXTRA-CREDIT—MORE ON BURIDAN'S ASS

We have shown that Buridan's ass is not rational: if he were, he would choose not to starve (given that he prefers eating to starving). But, Buridan might object, what is his hapless donkey to do? He must have a sufficient reason to choose this bale rather than that one: and given that the two are by hypothesis identical in all relevant qualities, he cannot do so. Perhaps then there is no rational alternative available and the paradox proves that in the situation described, there cannot be a perfectly rational agent.

We suggest that the example does not show so drastic a consequence. Rather, what it brings into question is the assumption that a perfectly rational agent must have a sufficient reason for deciding between two alternatives, under any description of these alternatives. The donkey does not have to be able to come up with a reason for choosing one bale over the other, in order to be rational. In this case, in fact, he would be irrational to waste time in a futile attempt to do so. (Don't worry if you find this section difficult: it is not essential and is included here just because the topic is interesting.)

DEMONSTRATED PREFERENCE ONCE MORE

Because demonstrated preference is so important in Austrian economics, let's return to it one more time. From the viewpoint of someone watching someone else act, every action shows a preference. If I see you throw down this book in disgust, then I know that doing so is your most highly preferred alternative.

From the "outside" viewpoint of another actor, the concept of indifference doesn't arise. All that one sees are particular actions, never a state of indifference.

THE BASIS OF MARGINAL UTILITY

If we were to acquire more and more units of a good, we would put them to less and less valuable uses. Another way of saying this is that the usefulness, or utility, of the last unit of a good decreases, the more units of a good we have at a given time. This principle is the famous law of diminishing marginal utility. (The marginal unit, to repeat, is the last unit.)

Unfortunately, some economists misunderstand the reasoning that establishes the principle of diminishing marginal utility. They think it rests on a psychological law, called the satiation of wants. Imagine that you have a sudden craving for ice cream. You accordingly march off to your favorite ice-cream store and proceed to gulp down one ice cream after another. Eventually, you will find that the joy of more ice cream wears off. If you keep eating ice cream, you will sooner or later reach a point at which you don't want any more. (People who work in ice-cream stores, who can have as much ice cream as they want, often get thoroughly sick of it.)

According to some economists, the lessening of wants explains diminishing marginal utility. As you get more of a good, you will derive less pleasure, or utility, from it. The nineteenth-century economist Heinrich Gossen, whom Werner Sombart termed a "brilliant idiot," was one of the first to develop this line of thought.

By now, you should be able to give the Austrian response. In praxeology, we are trying to deduce what follows from the concept of action. "Satiation of wants," if true, is a psychological generalization about people. It does not follow from the concept of action that your desire for ice cream will, after a while, diminish and fade away.

Whether this "law" obtains is an empirical matter: to find out about it, we would have to investigate the preferences of various people through psychological analysis. If we did, we would find that the law of diminishing marginal utility often turns out to be false. You might find that you get more of a "high" from the second or third ice cream than from the first. (In my own case, diminishing satisfaction would set in only at a very much larger number, if ever.)

In any event, psychological considerations of this sort do not concern us in economics. Diminishing marginal utility follows from the praxeological principle that people satisfy their most highly-valued ends first. It is not dependent on the results of any empirical investigations.

1. **Look up the treatment of Gossen in Joseph Schumpeter's *History of Economic Analysis* (Oxford: Oxford University Press, 1996), and give a brief report about him.**

2. **What would the "Chicago School" economists say about the basis of this law of diminishing marginal utility?**

*Joseph Schumpeter
1883–1950*

AN OBJECTION ANSWERED

We hope that you noticed that one comment made above about satiation of wants raises a problem. We said that you might get more enjoyment from a second ice cream than from your initial indulgence. Doesn't this contradict diminishing marginal utility, which tells us that the utility of the last unit of a good always decreases?

No, it does not. I'm afraid we must be repetitious once again. What we have been considering are the uses to which an actor proposes, at a particular time, to put different units of a good. These uses are ranked ordinally. (Aren't you getting sick of my saying this? You'd be surprised how many people don't get it.) Psychological estimates of pleasure—how much of a "bang" you get out of particular acts of consumption—don't concern us at all.

Let's apply this point to the ice-cream example. Each time you face the decision to eat another ice cream, you obviously have two alternatives before you. (We assume that you don't have other uses for ice cream besides eating it.) At each time, you will act to satisfy your most highly valued preference. How "satiated" or full you feel may well affect what choice you make: but satiation is not directly part of the analysis of marginal utility at all. In fact, since by hypothesis there is only one use for each unit of ice cream, the example probably isn't a very good one to illustrate marginal utility.

A better example would be one in which you had several different uses of the ice cream on your scale of preferences, in addition to eating the ice cream now: e.g., storing it, giving it to a friend, etc. With each additional unit, you will satisfy a less highly ranked preference. Of course, there is a complication. Your preference scale might look something like this:

- **EAT TWO ICE CREAMS**
- **EAT ONE ICE CREAM AND STORE ONE**
- **EAT ONE ICE CREAM**
- **STORE ONE ICE CREAM**

The alternative uses of the good do not have to describe qualitatively different uses. All you need for a preference scale is a specification of uses of a good. In this scale, two units of ice cream are treated, for the first two preferences, as a single use.

THE RELEVANT UNIT

What is crucial, then, is the uses to which you propose to put a good. These uses are subjective: they depend on your preferences. If you didn't have a preference scale like the one just given, but instead just considered each new decision whether to eat a new ice cream as a separate choice, then you would always be concerned with one unit of ice cream. (In suggesting that the ice-cream case was not a good one to illustrate the diminishing marginal utility, we were assuming that the actor considered only single units of ice cream, with a single use. It is this fact that "lops off" the scale of preference.)

It is important not to fall into fallacy here. Because the uses of a good depend on subjective preferences, and because these uses determine what you will consider relevant amounts of the good, it does not follow that the good itself is subjective.

You have certain uses for ice cream. But ice cream is a real physical good, "out there" in the world. You don't create it by your act of preference. In like manner, two units of ice cream, are, for part of the scales of preference that I gave, the relevant alternative to be chosen. But this preference scale does not determine what constitutes a physical quantity of ice cream. That, once more, is a matter of fact.

Some supposed Austrians, the so-called "radical subjectivists," get this point wrong. They think that because preferences are subjective, the good itself—the object of the preference—is also subjective. This of course does not follow. A few goods are states of mind—e.g., particular feelings that one aims to induce; but most economic goods are "physical items"—"stuff," if you will. (Complications that arise with money and credit are here ignored.)

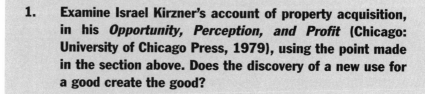

1.   Examine Israel Kirzner's account of property acquisition, in his *Opportunity, Perception, and Profit* (Chicago: University of Chicago Press, 1979), using the point made in the section above. Does the discovery of a new use for a good create the good?

EXTENSION OF MARGINAL UTILITY

The section just given was rather complicated. Let's get back to something simple—oranges. In the example of different uses of oranges, we were concerned, of course, with a single good. All of our examples have so far been of this sort.

But an actor usually does not have to decide on alternative uses of one good. He normally has a variety of goods at his disposal that must be assigned to varying uses. Given, say, that he has a choice between acquiring an orange, an apple, and a set of brass knuckles, what will he do?

The answer is straightforward. He will put the alternative uses of all the different goods on a single preference scale. Faced with a decision to acquire various units of different goods, he will in each case act to satisfy his highest ranking preference.

For each good, the law of diminishing marginal utility will apply. As more units of a good are acquired at a given time, they will be assigned to less valuable uses.

TWO KINDS OF EXCHANGE

The example we have been concerned with so far involves only one person. We have spoken, e.g., of an individual's scale of preferences. This part of economics is called Crusoe economics, after the character Robinson Crusoe in Daniel Defoe's novel. (Please do not call this "Caruso economics.")

Most economics, however, consists of studying actions that involve relations among two or more people. Here a distinction is crucial. One way you can deal with someone is by force or its threat. You want my giant stuffed teddy bear, so you grab it from me. Or you threaten to clobber me if I don't hand it over to you. In a related way, you might use fraud to obtain what you want. You might tell me that you will give me a real bear if I hand over the teddy bear, when you in fact have no intention of doing so.

As we'll see later, some parts of economics deal with force and fraud (the chapter on the monetary system will make this clear). But the main body of economics deals with voluntary, uncoerced action—action that does not involve force, the threat of force, or fraud.

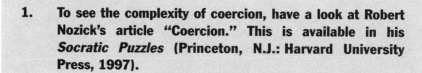

1.   **To see the complexity of coercion, have a look at Robert Nozick's article "Coercion." This is available in his** *Socratic Puzzles* **(Princeton, N.J.: Harvard University Press, 1997).**

MUTUAL BENEFIT FROM TRADE

If an action among two or more people is voluntary, a crucial fact about it at once follows. Since an actor always chooses his most highly valued alternative, he will not voluntarily engage in an action unless he would rather do so than refrain.

The preceding paragraph was too textbooky. Let's try again. Suppose I have an orange and you have an apple. I propose that we exchange our possessions: I will give you my orange if you will give me your apple.

If I propose doing this, I would rather exchange my orange for your apple than keep my orange. If you accept, you would rather exchange your apple for my orange than retain your apple.

For most purposes, we can assume that neither you nor I attach special value to the act of exchange as such. What each of us wants from our exchange are the goods he will get. If so, we can simplify the preferences in our case. I would rather have an apple than an orange and you would rather have an orange than an apple. In any voluntary exchange, the parties rank the goods exchanged in a different order on their preference scales. Suppose both our preference scales looked like this:

1 ORANGE
1 APPLE

Obviously, no exchange would take place. Suppose my preference scale looks like this:

1 APPLE
1 ORANGE

Then, if you have the reverse preference, I have oranges, and you have apples, a mutually beneficial trade can take place. No voluntary trade will take place unless all parties to the trade expect to benefit. And to benefit from an exchange, the parties must order their preferences differently. As we shall see in the next chapter, these facts play a crucial role in explaining prices.

Demand and Supply

4

Chapter 4
Demand and Supply

Long before now, you will have thought that this is a very strange economics book. Everybody knows that economics can be reduced to a pair of words: "demand" and "supply." Yet we have so far said nothing about them. Is this book a fraud?

In fact, we have not forgotten about demand and supply. (You probably guessed this if you read the chapter title.) These two concepts indeed are vital to economics, but you will be able to understand them much better now that you know something about utility.

Let's return to our favorite example: suppose I offer you one apple in exchange for one orange. We know that I would rather have one orange than one apple: otherwise, it would be foolish for me to offer an exchange. Similarly, you prefer one apple to one orange.

But we have so far left a key question without an answer. Why does one apple exchange for one orange? Why not one apple for two oranges? Or three apples for two oranges? (Obviously, the question we wish to pose is: why do exchanges take place in the real world at the ratio they do? The one apple–one orange exchange is just an example we have made up.)

> **1.** To reiterate, the problem is this: I have apples, and you have oranges. I prefer one orange to one apple, and you have the reverse preference. Each of us can benefit from an exchange. But what determines the ratio at which an exchange will take place?

The example given does tell us what the ratio of exchange must be. Since I prefer one orange to one apple, and you prefer one apple to one orange, apples and oranges will be exchanged on a one-for-one basis.

The answer to our question may disappoint you. In the example, we lack enough information to tell at what ratio the goods will exchange. True enough, both you and I will benefit if we exchange one apple for one orange. But suppose you ask for two apples in return for giving up an orange? As long as you value apples, you will be better off with two apples than one. I, of course, would rather surrender only one apple, so long as I value apples. (Remember, I did not say that I don't value apples, but rather that I prefer one orange to one apple.)

Your demand for two apples poses a problem for me. Would I rather have one orange than two apples? If I would, then I may accept your offer: if not, I will reject it. But, I may think, why should the terms of trade be shifted to your advantage in this way? Why not exchange one apple for two oranges? Or three?

A crucial asymmetry arises. Consider any suggested exchange ratio. If you would rather keep what you have than trade under these terms, no exchange will take place. But, if you would rather have the good you are offered, it does not follow that an exchange will take place at that ratio.

Confused? Let's try again. Someone proposes an exchange:

1 apple for 1 orange   (You have oranges)

If you would rather have one orange than one apple, no trade will take place. If you would rather have one apple than one orange, a trade will take place. But, the trade may not be at that ratio.

1 apple for 1 orange   2 apples for 1 orange

1 apple for 2 oranges   2 apples for 10 oranges

All of these ratios are consistent with your preferring one apple to one orange. We can't tell just from this preference how many apples it will take to get one orange.

1.   **In the last sentence, why don't we need to add "or how many oranges it will take to get one apple" in order to be complete?**

2.   **Give examples from your own experience in which you have traded one thing for another. If you traded one egg for one box of BB-gun pellets, would you expect exchanges of these items by your classmates to take place on the same terms?**

So far, economic theory hasn't told us much. We know that an exchange will take place if, and only if, both parties to it expect to benefit. Is that all? Fortunately, we can often go further. Let's get back to apples and oranges. It might turn out that you have a more detailed preference scale:

2 apples

1 apple

2 oranges

1 orange

Let's also suppose that you have four oranges and zero apples. Let's further assume that whenever you have a choice between acquiring one apple or one orange, you prefer the apple. I have four apples and zero oranges. I now offer to exchange apples for oranges with you at the rate of one apple for one orange. Obviously, you will be better off trading all your oranges for apples at this price. (By price, we mean the amount of a good you must give up to obtain one unit of another good that you want. It is vital to realize that price does not just mean what you as a buyer have to give up to get what you want. The goods that the seller receives are his price. Each party to an exchange is both "buyer" and "seller.") Can we now say that you and I will trade apples for oranges on a one-for-one basis?

If you answered that this follows, you have not been paying attention.

1. **See whether you can anticipate why we can't draw this conclusion about the ratio of exchange.**

2. **If you are given the apple price of oranges, show how you can at once obtain the orange price of apples.**

As you have no doubt anticipated, the case just given follows the same pattern as our earlier discussion. We know that, at a ratio of one apple for one orange, you will be better off (given your preference scale) to trade all your oranges for apples.

It's crucial to note the parentheses "(given your preference scale)." Remember, when you exchange, you are concerned with the marginal unit: would you rather have one apple or one orange? (We assume you are exchanging only single oranges and single apples.)

As you add more apples, the value of each added apple tends to fall. (Remember the law of diminishing marginal utility.) In like manner, as you surrender oranges, you will have to give up more and more valuable uses for your oranges. The value of the marginal unit will tend to go up, as your stock of oranges goes down.

Thus, the law of diminishing marginal utility plays a key role in fixing the limits of exchange. I have assumed that you always value one apple over one orange just to simplify the example. But, to return to our example, why should you accept the offered terms of exchange? Why not demand two apples for each orange? Remember, you value oranges: other things being equal, you will prefer to retain as many oranges as you can.

> **1.**   **"Sure, you can try for a better price. But then nothing stops the apple seller from trying to get a price more favorable to him. Given your preference scale, bargaining will tend toward a one-for-one price." What's wrong with this response?**

Well, so what? We have made a fuss about describing your preferences in more detail, but we seem to have made no progress. We still don't know what the price is. Will it help if my preference scale is filled in? Not in this example:

2 oranges

1 orange

2 apples

1 apple

Here my preferences are exactly the reverse of yours. I will be better off if I trade all my apples for your oranges; and you will be better off if you trade your oranges for my apples; but we do not know at what price the exchange will take place.

In this example, the ratio of exchange is indeterminate: any price that results in your getting all the apples and my getting all the oranges will make us both better off.

1. Economic theory can't tell us what the price will be, in cases like this. How do you suppose the price is actually determined?

2. What is meant by calling someone a good bargainer? In cases of indeterminate pricing, how can you obtain the ratio of exchange that is to your best advantage?

Again, you may ask: What's the point? We still have not come up with a way to determine price. But bringing in your preference scale has told us something. We know how many apples you will exchange for oranges, at a given price.

And sometimes, we can go further. Suppose the preference scales are as follows (As before, you start with four oranges and I with four apples):

YOU	2 APPLES
	1 APPLE
	2 ORANGES
	1 ORANGE

	2 ORANGES	
	2 APPLES	ME
	1 ORANGE	
	1 APPLE	

Just as before, I will be better off trading all my apples for your oranges at a ratio of one apple for one orange, and so will you. (Remember, we are using as assumption here: you always prefer one apple to one orange and I always prefer one orange for one apple.) But suppose you are not content. You demand two apples for each orange. Since I would rather have two apples than one orange, I will refuse to sell you any apples at this price. We can thus get a limit to the ratio of exchange. The apple price of oranges will be below two. Our scales allow some room for bargaining, but less than in the previous example.

> **1.   In the example, can we derive a limit to the orange price of apples? That is, if I demand two oranges for each apple, will I "price myself out of the market"? How about three oranges for each apple?**

?

Now matters become more interesting. (I realize this is not a strong claim.) Suppose that, while you and I have immersed ourselves in apples and oranges, other pairs of your classmates have been doing so as well. (Haven't they got anything better to do? They should be studying economics!) Each ratio of exchange of apples and oranges will depend on the preference scales of the two parties involved in it. Remember that the exchange-ratio may not be fully determined by these preference scales.

If we confine ourselves to separate two-person exchanges, the prices are likely to differ. Suppose I despise apples and would, if necessary, give them away. Your classmate Billy Carter, who also starts with four apples, just barely is willing to surrender an apple in order to get an orange. It is likely that I will be willing to give you more apples to get an orange than Billy will give to his trading partner, Colonel Kadaffi, for the same purpose.

Now for the good part. What happens once all these prices become known? I have been willing to give up four apples to get one orange; but I find that your friendly classmate, the Colonel, asks only one apple in return for one orange. I will shift my business to him. For similar reasons, though, he will shift from trading with Billy to trading with me (no doubt driving Billy to drink). Each person will shift trading partners until he can no longer secure a better price by doing so. In each market (an area in which buyers and sellers have ready access to each other and the various rates of exchange are known to all) a process of competition between people anxious to secure trade will tend to bring about a single price for

each good. This is termed the law of one price and is a basic principle of economics.

In real world markets, something else usually speeds this process of adjustment along. Some people are good at spotting differences in exchange ratios. By taking advantage of these discrepancies, they can secure gains for themselves. Suppose that someone, call him Arthur Arbitrageur, sees the difference in exchange ratios in the example just given.

Arthur, we assume, starts with four apples and has no interest in exchanging any of them for oranges. (Oranges just don't do it for him.) He sees, though, that if he can somehow get his hands on oranges at the Colonel's price, he is in luck. Once he does so, he can then come to me and exchange his oranges for apples. Suppose he starts with one apple. He exchanges it with the Colonel for one orange. He then buttonholes me and gets four apples for the orange he did not want for its own sake. He in effect has the use of a machine for transforming one apple into four.

Alas for him he cannot use the machine indefinitely. Other people will get into the act; and, in a way that we will examine in more detail below, a price will be established at which these gains cannot be obtained. These gains are called arbitrage profits, and persons who engage in them are called arbitrageurs.

?

1. **Suppose I anticipate Arthur's scheme. I lower the number of apples I am prepared to offer for one orange. How will the law of one price be affected?**

2. **Suppose a market has no arbitrageurs. Will the law of one price still operate?**

We have sketched, in a general way, how a price is determined, given a number of exchangers, each of whom has a preference scale for various quantities of two goods. Let's look at the process in more detail. Before doing so, I must issue a warning: here those dread monsters, demand and supply curves, enter the scene. (Since I am ungeometrical to an acute degree, they will not long detain us.)

Before doing so, though, we need to recall two principles: (1) you prefer more of a good to less; and (2) as you acquire more units of a good, you will put them to less valuable uses. (The second principle is the law of marginal utility.)

Now to the main business: given your preference scale, we can list how much of a good you will want at a given price. Here is an example:

At a price of five apples per orange, you want zero oranges

At a price of four apples per orange, you want one orange

At a price of three apples per orange, you want two oranges

At a price of two apples per orange, you want three oranges

At a price of one apple per orange, you want four oranges

1.   **Construct a preference scale that is consistent with this list.**

2.   **For any good you would like to acquire (e.g., a BB gun, a poster of Michael Jordan) construct a schedule of prices like the one above.**

Since this list tells how many oranges you want at each (apple) price, it is called the demand schedule for oranges. The example was just made-up; but we were not free to use just any numbers. All demand schedules must display certain general properties.

Why? Obviously, because the demand schedule is derived from a preference scale; and the preference scale must obey certain laws. (What are they?) If the preference scale must have certain characteristics, this causes the demand schedule to have certain other characteristics.

Put in another way; if a given demand schedule is possible, then there must be a possible preference schedule from which it can be derived. Some demand schedules do not meet this requirement. Therefore, they are not possible.

1.   **Sketch the argument type followed by the reasoning of the last paragraph. Is this form of argument valid? (Look at Chapter One for an explanation of what "valid" means.)**

Let's look at an example. Suppose this is your demand schedule:

At a price of five apples per orange, you want five oranges

At a price of four apples per orange, you want four oranges

At a price of three apples per orange, you want three oranges

Is this demand schedule possible? Well, what preference schedule would underlie it?

It would be one in which the more apples you had to give up to get an orange, the more oranges you would want. That is, on your scale, as you surrender more apples in trade, the value of apples to you falls. If you have to give up five apples to obtain one orange, then you will give up twenty-five apples to obtain five oranges, since on your preference scale, at this price:

5 ORANGES

25 APPLES

> **1.   Explain why this ranking must be part of your preference scale, in the indicated circumstances.**

But if you need give up only three apples to obtain one orange, you will want only three oranges. On your scale, at this price:

6 APPLES

5 ORANGES

This ranking holds because at the indicated price you will not make the trade. You prefer three oranges to fifteen apples, at a three apples per one orange price, but no more.

Thus, as you give up more apples, the value of apples falls. But this contradicts the law of diminishing marginal utility. As you gain more units of a good, the value of the last unit decreases, since you will put it to a less valuable use. Thus, as you lose units of a good, the value of the units you have left rises. Then, contrary to our hypothesis, as the price of oranges rises, you should be willing to give up fewer apples, not more.

And there is an easier way to demonstrate that this demand schedule contradicts the law of diminishing marginal utility. As you get more oranges, they will be demoted to less valuable uses. Then, as you obtain more oranges, you should be willing to give up less for them. But, on the rogue demand schedule, you want more oranges the higher the price. That is, you are willing to give up more for an orange when you get more oranges. And this cannot be true.

?

> **There is a much easier way to demonstrate that the assumed demand schedule is impossible. We first have the preference:**
> **5 oranges**
> **25 apples**
>
> **But we also have the preference:**
> **16 apples**
> **5 oranges**
>
> **We thus obtain:**
> **16 apples**
> **25 apples**
>
> **But this is impossible, so long as oranges are a good at all. You always prefer more of a good to less. What is wrong with this argument? (Hint: How do you derive the last preference?)**

EXTRA-CREDIT SECTION

Even if the argument just given did show an inconsistency in the preference scale, this would not suffice to show a logical contradiction. A preference is not an assertion; and it is not contradictory to hold inconsistent preferences. (It's usually not a good idea to do so, though.) If you prefer 5 oranges to 25 apples, but 16 apples to 5 oranges, at the same price, you commit no logical fallacy.

1.   **Look up the discussion of intransitive preferences in
      Human Action.**

?

LAW OF DEMAND

We have gone to a lot of trouble, but the result of our inquiry
can be summed up very simply. At a lower price, the quantity
demanded will be greater. This is the law of demand.

Now for that bitter pill, geometry. On a diagram with price and
quantity demanded of a good as the coordinates, we can show what
quantity will be demanded at a given price, and vice-versa.

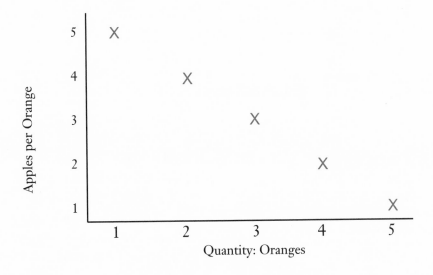

Figure 1. Price and Quantity

Here is an example:

In this diagram, at a price of five apples, one orange will be demanded; at a price of four apples, two oranges, etc. If we connect the points, we obtain the famous demand curve:

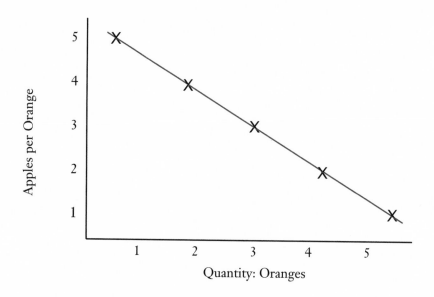

Figure 2. Demand Curve

You will see diagrams like this in practically all books about economic theory. But one note of caution is necessary. The points have been connected just because it is often convenient for purposes of illustration to do this. People make price–quantity decisions only in response to discrete units of a good; thus many points on the curve do not represent actual preferences of the demander. The question, e.g., how many apples will someone give up for one orange plus an undetectably small part of another orange may have no answer.

We have looked at things from the standpoint of the owner of apples who demands oranges. But what about the person who owns oranges and responds to this demand? He supplies oranges to the demanders.

Just as we did for the demander, so we can draw up a supply schedule, e.g.;

At a price of five apples per orange, I will supply five oranges
At a price of four apples per orange, I will supply four oranges
At a price of three apples per orange, I will supply three oranges

The higher the price, the more oranges I will make available: this is an instance of the law of supply.

1.   Why is the Law of Supply true?

I hope you found the easy way to answer this question. You could go through the same complicated rigmarole I did earlier, bringing in the Law of Marginal Utility. But you don't have to. Once we know the law of demand is true, it follows that the law of supply is true also. My supply schedule for oranges fixes my demand schedule for apples, and vice-versa. If I will supply five oranges at a price of five apples per orange, then I will demand five apples at a price of 1 to 5 orange per apple. These are just two ways of stating the identical exchange ratio.

1.   Work out the supply schedule for all the values of the demand schedule given in the example.

2.   Give an example of an impossible supply schedule.

A supply curve can be drawn:

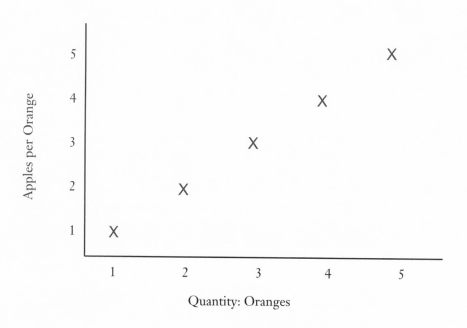

Figure 3. Supply Curve

The higher the price, the greater the quantity supplied. (The same warnings about the artificial nature of the curve that we mentioned earlier also apply here.)

Demand and supply curves do not have to curve just like the ones we have drawn here. Sometimes demand does not change much as price goes down:

This is termed an inelastic demand curve.

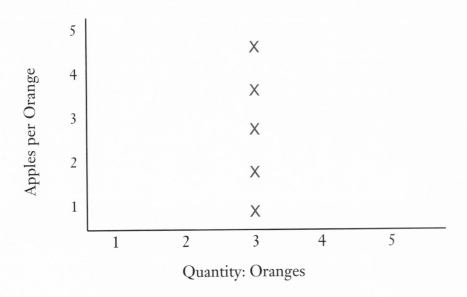

Figure 4. Inelastic Demand Curve

Similarly, supply can be fairly non-responsive to price changes. And the opposite circumstance may also obtain. The quantity demanded (and supplied) may be very responsive to price changes.

Here, a slight decline in price sharply increases quantity demanded; and a slight decline in price radically decreases quantity supplied. These are called elastic curves.

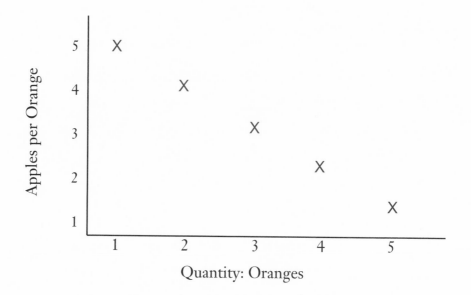

Figure 5. Elastic Demand Curve

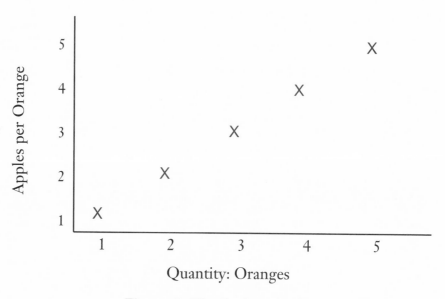

Figure 6. Elastic Supply Curve

We won't be going into much detail about the curvature of the demand and supply curves. But if you forget all else, you need to keep in mind two fundamental rules: the demand curve cannot slope downwards to the left, and the supply curve cannot slope downward to the right.

This can only be a demand curve, and

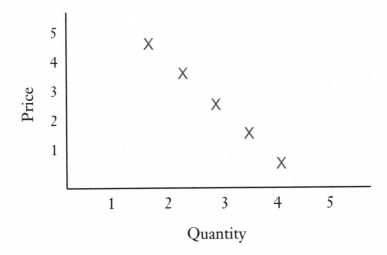

Figure 7. Demand Curve

this can only be a supply curve.

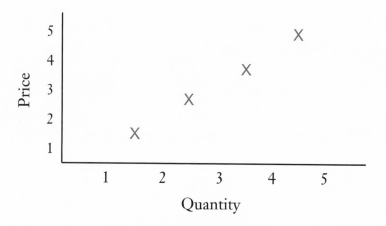

Figure 8. Supply Curve

Now we can complicate matters in an interesting way. Suppose we put the demand and supply curve for oranges, as priced in apples, on a single diagram. Then, we might get something like this:

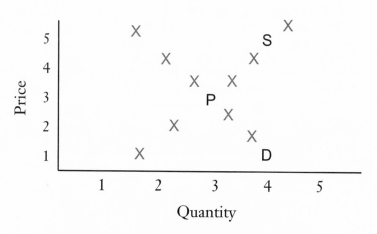

Figure 9. Demand and Supply Curve

Here the demand and supply curves intersect at point P.

So what? Here quantity demanded equals quantity supplied. At higher prices, more will be supplied than is demanded. Since the supplier would like to sell his excess stock, he will have an incentive to lower his price.

Similarly, at a price lower than the point of intersection, more will be demanded than will be supplied. Demanders would like to get more of the good than they are able to and will tend to bid up the price.

Only at the point of intersection will there be no tendency to bid the price up or down. This point is called the equilibrium, or market clearing, price.

> **1.   In what circumstances will suppliers like to sell their excess stock, given that to do so they must lower their asking price? They will sell more units at the lower price; but they will gain less per unit. When will this be to their advantage?**

So far, we have given demand and supply curves for individuals — my demand curve for apples, your demand curve for oranges, etc. But we can now apply a result that we reached earlier in this chapter. Remember our old friend Arthur Arbitrageur? (Actually, he is no more than a passing acquaintance of mine.) We showed that on a market, a single price tends to be established: this is the law of one price.

Do not be confused by the phrase "law of one price." The "law" does not act as some mysterious entity that establishes a single price. Rather, the law is a consequence of competition. Because the demanders compete by bidding for the same good, we can add their demands competition produces the law of one price.

One fact that usually speeds up getting to one price is expectations. Buyers want to avoid excess demand, and sellers have a parallel aversion to excess supply. They both will have an incentive to offer what they expect to be the market-clearing price. No law guarantees their expectations will be accurate; but, on a free market, experienced traders tend to be good at their jobs.

Because of this law, we can construct demand and supply curves that differ from those we have learned about. For each demander and supplier in the market, we have a demand and supply schedule. These schedules tell us how much a person will demand or supply at a given price.

We can add together the demand and supply schedules to obtain total demand and supply schedules for the market. From these, we can derive demand and supply curves, just as we did for individuals' demand and supply curves. Why can we do this? Since we know that all the exchangers will end up at the same price, we can treat the buyers and sellers as if they were all part of a single giant purchase and sale.

These demand and supply curves differ in a crucial respect from the demand and supply curves we have previously studied. Individuals' demand and supply schedules, the bases for drawing the curves, are determined by scales of preference. But there is no preference scale that corresponds to the sums of the demand and supply curves. The price is in fact close to the preferences of the marginal buyer and seller; but they are particular individuals. A preference scale corresponds only to the demand and supply of persons.

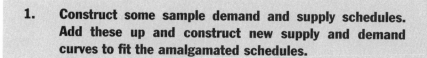

1. **Construct some sample demand and supply schedules. Add these up and construct new supply and demand curves to fit the amalgamated schedules.**

2.   ***Extra-credit:*** **See whether you can set out explicitly the steps in the justification for adding together the demand and supply schedules. Note that for the argument to go through, you must assume that people's preferences do not change during arbitrage transactions.**

Now that we have explained demand and supply, you may be tempted to close this book. After all, economics is "supply and demand"—isn't it?—so what more is left? Do not give in to temptation; you need to grasp a crucial fallacy. This fallacy is easy to fall into; but, fortunately, you can readily avoid it.

The demand curve slopes downward to the right: if at a lower price, demand is greater. Perfectly true: but here lies danger. What is greater is the quantity of the good demanded. But an increase in demand may also designate a shift of the entire demand curve. A diagram will show this:

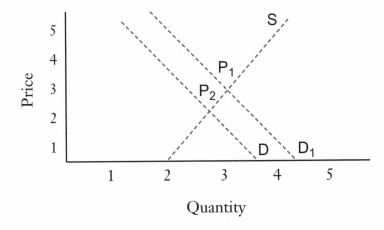

Figure 10. Supply Curve Shift

In the first diagram, the price has been lowered from p1 to p2. At p2, the quantity demanded is greater than at p1. But the demand curve, as a whole, has stayed constant; it is the supply curve that has shifted. In the second diagram, by contrast, the entire demand curve has shifted to the right, and the supply curve is unchanged. Note that this increase in demand results in a higher price, not a lower one. To avoid ambiguity, an increase in demand should be used only to designate a movement of the whole curve; the other change is one in quantity demanded.

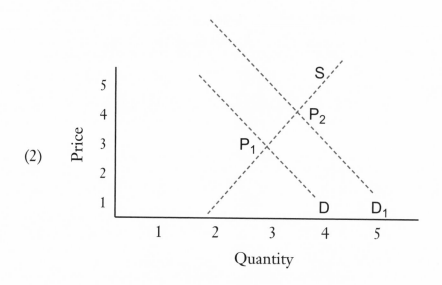

Figure 11. Demand Curve Shift

To sum up in an easy-to-remember catchphrase: Don't confuse movement along the demand (or supply) curve with a shift of the entire curve.

1. **Diagram the distinctions between (1) a fall in quantity demanded and a lowering of the entire demand curve; (2) a rise or fall in quantity supplied and the appropriate shift in the supply curve. (You knew this was coming, didn't you?)**

SUMMARY

This chapter, I fear, has been rather long and tedious. If you remember only one thing in it, let it be this: Value is subjective. Individuals' assessments of goods determine prices.

In the next chapter, we shall see what happens to economics if this point is ignored.

The Labor Theory of Value

Chapter 5
The Labor Theory of Value

The discussion of the previous chapter generates a major problem. In the first part of the chapter, bargaining on price as subject to few constraints was presented. If you would rather have an apple of mine than an orange of yours, and my preference is the reverse, then an exchange will benefit us both. But, we found, little could be said about the ratio of exchange. It might be one apple for one orange, two apples for one orange, three oranges for one apple, etc. Almost all was left in darkness.

But, later in the chapter, things seemed different. Here, determining the price appeared easy: you simply draw the demand curve, draw the supply curve, and see where they intersect. What could be easier?

Do we have a contradiction? Let's have a closer look:

1. Apart from the results of bargaining by those actually engaged in an exchange, we cannot determine the ratio at which the items exchange.

2. Given the demand and supply curves of the exchangers, we can easily determine the exchange ratio: it is the point at which the curves intersect.

> **1.** **How about it? Is there a contradiction? Reread the discussion of the law of noncontradiction in Chapter One.**

?

WHY THERE IS NO CONTRADICTION

Fortunately for me, the two statements do not contradict each other. The first statement is categorical: it says that the ratio of exchange cannot be determined apart from the bargaining of the exchangers. The second statement, by contrast, is hypothetical: it says that if the demand and supply curves are given, then the price can be determined.

This enables us to escape contradiction. So long as the if-clause of the hypothetical is not realized, both statements can be true consistently.

Let's go over this again. (If you don't need to, feel free to omit this paragraph.) The hypothetical says what will happen if the demand and supply curves are given. It does not say that the curves are given. So long as the curves are not given, the statement makes no claim about how easy it is to determine the ratio of exchange. Thus it does not contradict the claim that the ratio is undetermined.

1. "But if the if-clause is never realized, the proposition is always false. Therefore, you have escaped contradiction only by withdrawing one of the statements you first made." What is wrong with this argument?

2. What would you have to add to the two statements to generate a contradiction?

3. Give other examples of two statements that (1) appear to be contradictory; (2) but in fact are not, because one of them is a hypothetical whose "if" clause is not realized.

DEMAND AND SUPPLY CURVES REVISITED

The solution to our paradox of course raises a new question. Why aren't demand and supply curves given in the real world? To answer this is easy, once we remember how demand and supply curves are constructed. As you will recall, to get a demand or supply curve, you must first have a demand or supply schedule. Therefore, if the demand or supply schedule is not fixed, neither is the demand or supply curve.

But we now face a new question. Why aren't the demand and supply schedules given in advance of bargaining? To answer this, we must return once more to praxeology. Remember what our aim is as students of economics. We are attempting to derive propositions from the axiom of action that illuminate our subject.

It does not follow from the action axiom that the demand and supply schedules must be fixed in advance. Perhaps you do know, before you start exchanging apples and oranges, how much of each good you will want at each price; but nothing requires this.

Can you see how this last remark requires a modification of what has gone before? It is not entirely right to say either that the ratio of exchange is indeterminate or that it is never the case that the demand and supply schedules cannot be fixed in advance. Rather, what we should say is that nothing requires these schedules to be fixed, from the standpoint of praxeology. We can then maintain, once more from the standpoint of praxeology, both of the statements we have insisted on: (1) the ratio of exchange is indeterminate (according to praxeology); and (2) if the supply and demand curves are given, the price is determined.

Another point reinforces our conclusion. Suppose you own peanuts, which you want to trade for my pictures of wrestling stars. (I'm tired of apples and oranges, aren't you?) You may (or may not) have in mind a schedule of how many peanuts you will offer for pictures of various wrestling stars. Either is consistent with the action axiom. Similarly, I may or may not have a schedule of proposed trades in my mind. But you cannot determine, by praxeology, whether I have such a schedule. If you have one, it does not follow that I do; and if you do not, I may have one all the same.

In Austrian economics, the preferences that we are concerned with are those demonstrated in action. If I offer one picture of Hulk Hogan for ten peanuts, then I prefer ten peanuts to one picture of the Hulkster; my offer shows this. The relative rankings of other combinations are, from the point of view of praxeology, irrelevant. What counts are the preferences actually expressed on the market: the others, "like the flowers that bloom in the spring, tra-la/Have nothing to do with the case."

Of course, you know whether you have a fixed preference scale, just as I know whether I have one. But neither scale is given, just by reasoning from the action axiom. From that point of view, one can just as well as assume that neither you nor I has a fixed scale of preferences.

Thus, all our talk of demand and supply curves is hypothetical. All that we are really given, strictly speaking, is the point at which the curves intersect: that is to say, the actual price in the purchase-sale transaction. (A famous British economist, Sir Dennis Robertson, emphasized this.)

If the curves are hypothetical, why use them? You should know the answer by now. Hypothetical reasoning is often extremely useful in science; in economics it is indispensable.

We so far have stressed that the curves are not really "out there": fixed preference scales, we have learned, need not exist. But we must not push the point too far. Some economists think that preferences do not exist except at the moment of action. (James Buchanan, a Nobel laureate in economics, holds this view.) We are not committed to it.

There is a misunderstanding that is easy to fall into here. In fact, I fell into it myself. Fortunately, an eminent Austrian economist called this to my attention. Go back to the apparent contradiction on the first page of this chapter. Note that it concerns whether we can determine the rate of exchange to two commodities.

If, as was argued above, an outside observer cannot determine this rate, it does not follow that the rate is indeterminate. Instead, it may be the case that the rate is fixed; but outside observers cannot know this.

The eminent economist who pointed this out to me contends that at the moment a trade takes place, the preference scales of all individuals involved are fixed. In his view, an individual may himself be unaware of his latent preference scale.

I'm not sure whether this is right: but the argument in the text does not exclude this position. Even if preference scales latently exist, we can only observe the results of bargaining. These scales are inaccessible.

Can you see why not? Once more, praxeology does not require the denial of this position. The claim that preferences are not "in the mind" but are to be found only in behavior is a philosophical doctrine. Whether it is true is not our function as economists to determine. Once more, we want to know what follows from the action axiom. Controversial philosophical theories should be avoided.

1. **Are market demand and supply curves also hypothetical? What argument shows this?**

2. **"It doesn't follow that action is always demonstrated in preference. Sometimes you do things, even though you really don't want to." How would an Austrian respond to this contention?**

Adam Smith
1723–1790

Karl Marx
1818–1883

ANOTHER ECONOMICS?

The approach to price and value that we have so far discussed, the subjective theory of value, has been developed since the 1870s. (It was advanced in the Middle Ages and Renaissance, but fell into eclipse during the nineteenth century.) Some economists look at value in a different way: these are members of the so-called classical school, which includes Adam Smith and David Ricardo.

In order to understand Austrian economics better, you will find it a big help to look at the classical doctrine. After we have done so, we shall then examine the radically different way Austrians look at the key element in the classical theory—cost of production.

We shall look at the classical theory in the form given it by its most controversial exponent—Karl Marx, the founder of "scientific socialism." He argued very systematically for his theory. We shall be able to use what we know already to help us see what is wrong with Marx's theory. And our examination brings with it another benefit. For much of the twentieth century, communist governments dominated a great part of the world. These regimes based themselves explicitly on Marx's theories. Wrong theories have an immense power to do damage.

1. Do a brief report on the life of Karl Marx. From what you can discover about his life, does he strike you as someone sincerely concerned with the welfare of humanity? You will find it useful to look at Paul Johnson's book, *Intellectuals* (New York: Harper Collins, 1990).

2. Identify the following and what they did: Friedrich Engels, Karl Kautsky, V.I. Lenin.

THE MARXIST ABCs

As we have learned, to say that exchange ratios, or prices, are determined by supply and demand leaves us with much up in the air. The supply and demand curves depend on individual preferences: they are fixed only to the extent the latter are.

Marx maintained that to be satisfied with this is the sign of superficial, "vulgar," economics. The task of theory is to discover the laws that underlie economic behavior.

He did not reject the subjective theory entirely. On one point, the theory was right. In order to have economic value, a good has to have utility. We wouldn't exchange apples and oranges (sorry—they are back again) unless we valued at least one of these goods. If kumquats have no use to me, I will not trade for them. So much Marx admitted; he was not, for once, bereft of common sense.

This fact enables us to see the fallacy in a common argument against Marx's theory. As we'll soon see, Marx explained the economic value of a good by the labor-hours needed to produce it. But what if someone spent an enormous amount of time making mudpies? No matter how much time he spent laboring on the mudpies, they are worthless: no one wants mudpies.

This objection leaves Marx unmoved. In order to be valuable, a good must have utility, or as Marx and the classics called it, use-value. Since mudpies have no utility, they are without economic value. This holds both for the Austrian and Marxist theories of value.

> **1.** **"If Marx admitted that only things with utility had economic value, then he is really a subjective value theorist too." What is wrong with this objection?**

WHY MARX IS NOT A SUBJECTIVIST

The answer to our inquiry is straightforward. Marx thought that in order to have economic value, a good must have utility. So far, he and the subjective school are at one. But now, Marx parts company from Austrian economics. Once a good passes the utility test, subjective value exits the scene. It has nothing more to do with determining the value of the good.

Why did Marx take this step? Oddly, he did so because he fully realized a basic truth we have already learned about subjective value. Subjective values are ordinal: I can say that I prefer one orange to one apple, but I can't say how much I prefer it. I cannot say one orange has so-and-so many more units of utility than one apple. Further, it is impossible to compare my preference for oranges with your preference: we can't make interpersonal utility comparisons.

Do you see why not? Each preference scale gives only the ordinal rankings of one individual:

ME	YOU
2 oranges	2 apples
1 orange	1 apple
2 apples	2 oranges
1 apple	1 orange

The question, how does my ranking of two oranges compare with your ranking of one apple? makes no sense. As we have defined preference, this question breaks the rules.

But just here is where the problem lies, according to Marx. Because use-value is subjective, it cannot be the basis of a science of value. The purpose of science is to come up with objectively true laws: subjective value cannot fill the requirement. Thus, out with it!

1. What basic error did Marx make about science in this line of reasoning?

2. Behaviorism, a movement in psychology, is analogous to Marx's rejection of subjectivism. Write a brief report on this movement.

3. "Since Marx admits that only goods with use-value have economic value, he has not banished subjectivism from his own theory. Thus, his theory fails by its own standards." How would Marx reply to this objection?

MARX'S SOLUTION TO HIS PROBLEM

How, then, can one arrive at a science of economic value? According to Marx, economic goods have another property besides use-value: exchange-value. If I own one apple, the apple not only meets certain wants of mine directly. It can be used to obtain other goods. Perhaps I can obtain one orange with it. (If I can't, many of this book's examples will be ruined.)

Exchange value, according to Marx, gives us the basis for a true science of value. Suppose one apple exchanges for one orange. Then, one apple = one orange. Here, to Marx, is the indispensable first step of science.

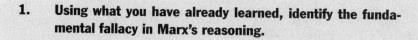

1.   Using what you have already learned, identify the fundamental fallacy in Marx's reasoning.

MARX'S BASIC MISTAKE

As I hope you have already spotted, the initial step of Marx's argument is mistaken. An exchange is not an equality, but a double inequality. If I trade one of my apples for one of your oranges, then I value one orange more than one apple, and you value one apple more than one orange. Otherwise, no exchange would take place.

Marx might counter our objection in this way. Granted that there is a double inequality, this applies only to use-value. But use value does not explain economic value. That task falls to exchange value, and here there must be an equality.

This reply exposes another basic mistake that Marx made. He assumes, wrongly, that exchange value exists entirely apart from use-value. In fact it does not. Why does an apple have an exchange-value? Because with it, I can secure an orange. And the extent of that value depends on how much I want oranges, and how much you want apples. Exchange-value comes from use-value or utility: it is not some sort of mystical entity that exists in its own right.

1.   **How might Marx reply to this objection? How in turn would an Austrian respond?**

2.   **What basic principles of praxeology does Marx's theory violate?**

?

MARX'S ERRORS ABOUT SCIENCE

Marx would probably respond to our point in this way: We are begging the question in favor of the subjective theory of value. But in fact we have not done so. We explained how exchange-value arises from subjective-value. What justification does Marx have for conjuring up "exchange-value" as an independent entity? This has not been derived from the axiom of action.

But is this a good objection against Marx? He, after all, makes no claim to be a praxeologist. Why should he be bound by that discipline's requirements? This line of defense, I am afraid, gives Marx no hope. Whatever his views about praxeology, he confronts a basic problem: he must justify his claim that exchange-value exists apart from use-value. And this he has not done.

MORE MARXIST MISTAKES

Marx might answer us this way: "You're looking in the wrong place. The justification for exchange-value just is that it enables me to come up with exact laws of value. I don't need any other support for introducing the concept."

Unfortunately for Marx, his attempt to derive exact laws of value fails. Let's go back to basics, i.e., apples and oranges. We have: One apple = one orange.

According to Marx, this means that one apple is identical to one orange. But, obviously, an apple is very different from an orange. How then can Marx assert that they are identical?

Nothing (or at least very little) was beyond Marx. He knew perfectly well that an apple is not identical with an orange: but there must be, he thought, some underlying entity in the apple and orange that is the same in both. Otherwise, there would be no equality: and without an equality, we could not derive laws of exchange.

Very well, then: one apple and one orange contain an identical element. What is it? According to Marx, it can only be labor. One apple exchanges for one orange because the same quantity of human labor is required to produce each of them.

BÖHM-BAWERK'S CRITICISMS

Eugen von Böhm-Bawerk, an outstanding Austrian economist who also served as Austrian Finance Minister in the early twentieth century, subjected Marx's argument to withering assault. He devoted two main works to Marx's economics: part of a chapter in his great treatise *Capital and Interest* and a separate short book called *Karl Marx and the Close of His System*.

Böhm-Bawerk located a gap in Marx's argument. Suppose we concede to Marx that there is an equality involved in exchange. And suppose we grant him that the equality entails an identity. Why does the identical element have to be labor? Why can't the common element be something else?

And labor seems an unpromising choice for the supposed common element. The value of some goods seems clearly not to depend on the labor time needed to produce them. Böhm-Bawerk noted that wine often increases in value the longer it is stored. The labor required to gather the grapes and turn them into wine contributes very little to the price of wine.

Eugen von Böhm-Bawerk
1851–1914

1. ***Extra-credit:*** **Give examples of other goods besides wine whose value doesn't depend on the labor required to produce them.**

2. **Marx argued that if there is an equality in an exchange, there must be an underlying identity that explains it. Was he right?**

ANOTHER FALLACY

Böhm-Bawerk pointed out an even more important fallacy in Marx's argument. Everyone knows that some people are much more efficient workers than others. You might be able to build a wooden bookend in a few hours, but it would take me several years to do it. Will my bookend be worth several times more than yours? Of course not! Economic value, then, does not depend on the labor time required to produce something.

Marx knew this. But, as we have already sufficiently seen, he almost never gave up one of his pet theories. To meet the difficulty, he said that it was not the labor required to produce a particular good that determined its value; rather, it was the labor "socially necessary" to produce items of that class. My bookend would not be unusually valuable, however long I took to construct it, because bookends typically do not require several years to make.

Here Böhm-Bawerk launched his criticism. What determines whether the amount of labor is socially necessary? Sometimes, as in my bookend example, the answer is obvious: we don't use the work of an incompetent as a criterion. But often it isn't obvious what to count as socially necessary. Should we adopt the least possible time it takes anyone to produce something as the standard? If not that, what?

Böhm-Bawerk noted that to solve this problem, Marx needed actual market prices. "Socially necessary" labor was the labor needed to produce goods at the market price. Those who required more labor than this to produce a good were not performing labor that was "socially necessary."

Can you see the flaw in Marx's method? As Böhm-Bawerk pointed out, Marx has reasoned in a circle. He claims that the market price of a good is determined by the labor socially necessary to produce it. He cannot then appeal to the good's market price in order to find out how much labor is socially necessary.

And the identical fallacy infects a related part of the theory. How can the labor hours required to produce one hour of a good be compared with the labor hours needed to make a good of a completely different type? How can my labor on this book be compared with Michael Jordan's labor on the basketball court? (And why does the result of the comparison have to place me at such a disadvantage?) How do you compare a surgeon's labor with a bricklayer's?

Unless Marx can arrive at a common measure of labor, he will not have a labor theory of value. He will be left with distinct types of labor, and he will be unable to explain how the ratio of exchange is determined when a good produced by one sort of labor is exchanged for a good produced by another.

See whether you can guess Marx's "solution." That's right: he argued that the many different varieties of labor could indeed be reduced to a common measure. And how was this to be done? Why, by reference to the market prices of the types of labor, of course! (Fortunately, I'm not going to explain the complicated way he tried to do this.)

Once more, Böhm-Bawerk identified the fallacy. To use market prices to reduce the types of labor to a common measure blatantly reasons in a circle. The fallacy Marx commits is exactly the same as the one of which he was guilty in defining "socially necessary" labor.

1. **Set out in detail the steps of the argument showing that Marx is guilty of circular reasoning in his account of measuring socially necessary labor.**

2. **Given the fallacies of Marx's theory, why do you think he advanced it? Couldn't he see the obvious difficulties of the theory?**

A FINAL ANOMALY

We have discussed a great many problems with Marx's labor theory. (If anyone says here, "Too many, and at too great length" the teacher should banish him from the classroom.) But suppose, for a moment, we put all these problems aside. What would then happen?

Strangely enough, we would still not have a theory that adequately explained price. And of this Marx was fully aware. He knew full well, and explicitly said, that goods do not in a capitalist economy exchange at their labor values! (His reasons, unfortunately, cannot be explained now because they involve parts of economics that haven't yet been covered here.)

The situation is almost too much to believe. Marx has gone to elaborate lengths to arrive at an allegedly scientific theory that will explain why goods exchange at the ratios they do. But his theory, on his own admission, does not do this. What gives?

Marx answered as follows: true, the labor theory does not explain actual prices. But given labor prices, the theory can show how actual prices are derived. Thus the theory is vindicated: it does explain price after all. Once more Marx met his nemesis in Böhm-Bawerk. In a way that we won't explain here, he showed that Marx's attempted derivation of real prices from labor values fails: the details just don't add up.

Rather than go into the technical details of Marx's derivation and Böhm-Bawerk's criticism, let us raise a more general issue. Suppose Marx could derive real prices from labor values. That is to say, suppose Marx's arithmetic was right: how much difference would this make? Marx's claim is that he can show what the "laws of motion" of capitalism really are. Others may linger at the surface: he will plumb the depths.

But how does deriving one figure from another meet this exacting requirement? An example will illustrate the problem. (Naturally, we return to oranges and apples):

One orange exchanges for one apple

In this circumstance, a 1:1 exchange ratio, the apple price of one orange is one apple. Given the apple price of oranges, we can at once derive the orange price of apples. But, in doing so, we have not shown that the apple price of oranges somehow underlies, is more basic than, the orange price of apples. To get a genuine explanation, more than a numerical derivation is needed.

As I hope you are convinced, the labor theory of value does not offer an acceptable alternative to the Austrian theory.

1. **What notion of scientific explanation did Marx rely on in his theory? Do you think his view was correct? Why not?**

2. **Look at the first few chapters of Marx's *Capital*, volume one, to get some idea of how elaborate his theory is.**

3. **How does praxeology respond to the issue of what constitutes a genuine explanation?**

Chapter 6
Price Controls

Long before now, you will probably have thought: Why bother with economics? In fact, some of you may have thrown this book aside. If so, get it back: we'll see in this chapter how economic theory helps us analyze policy issues.

> 1.   **"Prices are too high." What do you think this common complaint means?**
>
> 2.   **"Wages are too low." How does this frequent statement relate to the previous complaint?**

INTERFERENCE WITH THE MARKET

"Gasoline prices are outrageous: why not compel the oil companies to sell more cheaply? After all, they make vast sums in profit: it's not as if cutting their gains will send their stockholders to the poorhouse."

What will happen if, say, gasoline prices are lowered from $1.30 per gallon (the market price) to $1.00 per gallon? At the market price, every buyer can find a seller; and every seller a buyer.

105

Can you see from our previous chapters why this is true? One way to show this appeals to a special type of argument called a *reductio*. In a *reductio*, we assume that the contradictory of what we want to prove is true. We then show that this hypothesis leads to a contradiction. If so, the contradictory of our original hypothesis is true.

Confused? You should be. Let's have another look:

(1) We want to prove statement p.

(2) We show that not -p leads to a contradiction.

(3) This proves that p is true.

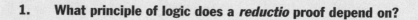

1.   What principle of logic does a *reductio* proof depend on?

WHAT IF BUYERS AND SELLERS DON'T MATCH?

We can use a *reductio* proof to show that at the market price, every buyer finds a seller and every seller a buyer. Suppose that at the market price of gasoline, $1.30 per gallon, there are more buyers than sellers (not-p). More people want to buy gasoline at that price than can be supplied. What will happen?

Obviously, the buyers will scramble to try to get the gasoline. This is why when there are "price wars" among gas stations, you usually have to wait in long lines. You will not be surprised to learn that people do not like to wait in line. Some buyers will then offer a higher price.

What happens at the new offer? Fewer buyers will want gasoline at the higher price but more sellers will be willing to offer gasoline for purchase. Eventually, supply and demand will balance.

1.   *Extra-credit:* which buyers will bid up the price?

2.   "The analysis given in the text does not work. In most market transactions, buyers do not offer a price. The seller sets the price. Unless the seller increases prices, then, prices will not rise." What's wrong with this objection? Show:
    (a) why the alleged fact that buyers do not
        raise prices is false;
    (b) why even if the alleged fact were true,
        the conclusion would not follow.

3.   *Super-extra credit.* Is the argument given in the text a strict *reductio* proof or just analogous to such a proof? If you can answer this question you are probably a ringer.

A BASIC RULE OF ECONOMICS

I have good news for you. If you have found the discussion of *reductio* proof confusing, you can understand the fundamental economic principle without explicit reference to it. All you have to remember is this: if there are more buyers than sellers at a given price, the price will rise; if there are more sellers than buyers at a given price, the price will fall. The market tends to balance buyers and sellers.

MARGINAL BUYERS AND SELLERS

All right: if there are more buyers than sellers, buyers will bid up the price (just to keep your hand in, state the analogous proposition that is true when there are more sellers than buyers).

But which buyers will do this? Obviously, economic theory cannot identify the specific buyers who will do this: it does not tell you that John Jones or John Elway will bid up the price.

?

1.   **Why not? Recall the discussion in an earlier chapter about praxeology. Economic theory deals in general propositions, not propositions about specific people. In economic history, we apply the general truths to specific situations by "filling in the blanks." We thus use theory to help us understand history; but history and theory are very different things.**

MARGINAL BUYERS AND SELLERS, CONTINUED

Economic theory, though, can tell us something about which buyers will bid up the price. Let's suppose that the price of gasoline is $1.00 per gallon and, at this price, more buyers than sellers exist.

Some buyers at the price of $1.00 per gallon will not be willing to pay higher prices. $1.00 per gallon is their limit. These are called marginal buyers. The buyers who offer higher prices will be those who are willing to pay more than $1.00 per gallon to get gasoline. As prices rise, marginal buyers are driven out.

As you might expect, a quite similar phenomenon holds true for supply. Suppose that at a price of $1.00 per gallon, there are more sellers than buyers: more people are willing to sell at that price than are willing to buy. What will happen? (Before reading the next paragraph, see whether you can work out the analysis yourself.)

At the price of $1.00 per gallon, we suppose, some sellers will not find buyers. Some sellers will be willing to sell at a lower price: they would be better off disposing of the gasoline at less than $1.00 per gallon, than not being able to sell all their gasoline at the higher price. Others, the marginal sellers, will exit the market. If they cannot get at least $1.00 per gallon, they don't want to sell gasoline.

Once again, the market matches buyers and sellers. At the new, lower price, say 80¢ per gallon (why not? it's my example and I'm free to make up the figures), there are neither sellers nor buyers who cannot trade as they wish.

1. **The marginal buyers and sellers, we have said, are those who, given an unfavorable small change in price, prefer not to trade. By what standard is this assessed? Who determines that someone would be better off trading than not trading?**

ENTER THE VILLAIN

Unfortunately, the state sometimes refuses to let well enough alone. Suppose the state decides that the price of gasoline is "too high." It imposes a price ceiling of $1.00 per gallon. It is illegal to charge more than this for gasoline. The market price, we suppose, is $1.30 per gallon.

What will happen? At the $1.00 per gallon price, more buyers than sellers exist. Not everyone who wishes to purchase gasoline can do so. The result is a shortage of gasoline.

If the free market were allowed to operate, the price would rise until the market price was reached. At $1.30 per gallon, the number of buyers and sellers would be equal.

?

1.   *Extra-credit:* **Do cases exist in which a price ceiling will not cause a shortage?**

CEILINGS AND SHORTAGES, CONTINUED

Oddly enough, the answer to the question just posed is yes. Suppose the price ceiling is higher than the market price. For example, the market price is $1.30 per gallon of gasoline and the government imposes a price ceiling of $1.60 per gallon. What will be the result?

That's right, nothing at all. The price ceiling will not stop buyers and sellers from reaching the market price. Thus, we can say that a price ceiling will either be useless or cause a shortage.

?

1.   **Why do you think that the government would ever impose a price ceiling above the market price?**

YET ANOTHER COMPLICATION

As you have no doubt by this time discovered, I like complications. It is not always true that a price ceiling above the market price has no effect. Can you see why not?

Buyers and sellers care not only about prices now, but also about their estimates of future price changes. Suppose I think that the market price of gasoline, absent government interference, will rise from its present $1.30 to $1.65. My expectations of the price change may influence how I now act. If I think that the expected rise will be blocked by the price ceiling, my course of action may well be different. Fortunately, you don't have to worry about this in introductory economics.

AND ANOTHER COMPLICATION

There is another case in which a price ceiling will not cause a shortage. Suppose, as before, that the government imposes a price ceiling of $1.00, when the market price is $1.30. A possible state of affairs is that preferences shift, so that the number of buyers and sellers match at $1.00 instead of $1.30. In other words, the ceiling induces shifts in preferences that "justify" it.

But we have only to mention this to see how unlikely this is to happen. Why would the government's action have this effect? Once more, we should keep the main point in mind, (while not ignoring the complications). A price ceiling will either be useless or cause a shortage.

1.   *Extra-credit:* **Can you work out a circumstance in which a price ceiling will induce a surplus (more sellers than buyers, at that price)?**

THE ETHICAL POINT

Price ceilings cause shortages; therefore, the government should not institute them. What could be more evident?

Well, the premise is true; the conclusion (in the author's judgment) is also true. But the conclusion does not follow from the premise.

> **1.** **Give other examples of arguments with true premises and a true conclusion, where the premises do not entail the conclusion. Note that in order to reason correctly, the conclusion must be validly deduced from the premises.**

ETHICS CONTINUED

But wait a minute. *Doesn't* the conclusion follow the premises? Surely, shortages are bad; and if a government program causes a bad state of affairs to happen, it is bad. Therefore, price ceilings are bad and the government ought to avoid them.

> **1.** **Using the previous discussion, can you see why the new argument does not show that the conclusion follows from the previously stated premises?**

EVEN MORE ETHICS

The answer should be obvious. The new argument does not show that the conclusion, the government shouldn't impose price controls, follows from the original premises because we have added a *new* premise. What is it?

"Shortages are bad." It is this that enables us to move from premises to conclusion. In general, you need an ought statement in the premises to justify an ought judgment in the conclusion. A value judgment will also do the trick.

1. **Give examples of value judgments.**

2. **"Since value judgments are subjective, no ought statements can be backed up by reason." Evaluate this claim.**

3. **Some philosophers deny that you always need an "ought" in one of your premises to get to an "ought" in the conclusion. Find out who some of these thinkers are, and give a brief account of their arguments. Why wouldn't their views require us to modify our conclusion about what follows from "price controls cause shortages?"**

MUCH ADO ABOUT VERY LITTLE?

Haven't we made too much fuss over a very minor point? After all, who doubts that shortages are bad? Perhaps some misanthrope enjoys depriving others of the goods they want; but, barring exceptional cases such as this, aren't we home free?

Indeed, don't we have here a partial solution to the so-called fact-value gap? Just add an obviously true value judgment. Compare the following:

- (1) YOU DO NOT WANT TO DIE BY POISONING
- (2) THAT GLASS OVER THERE CONTAINS POISON
- (3) YOU SHOULD NOT DRINK THE CONTENTS OF THAT GLASS

Premise (1) is a value judgment, but it is none the worse for that.

WHY WE ARE NOT HOME FREE

Unfortunately, we have not yet arrived at a good argument against price control. Can you see the problem? From "shortages are bad" and "price controls cause shortages," it does not follow that price control ought not to be instituted.

Why not? Let's consider a parallel argument:

- **(1) DENTISTRY CAUSES PAIN**
- **(2) PAIN IS BAD**
- **(3) DENTISTRY OUGHT TO BE OUTLAWED**

Obviously, something has gone wrong. Even though something has some bad results, it may still be worth doing. Its good consequences may outweigh its bad consequences. Thus, few advocates of price controls will welcome shortages. But they may think that the badness of shortages is outweighed by the alleged good effects of lower prices. Or they may try to cope with the shortages by other means.

An example of this strategy emerges in justifications of rationing. During wartime, consumer goods are in short supply. Some people think it is "unfair" to allow prices to rise; and to prevent shortages, the government issues ration books. You must have a ration card, in addition to the requisite money, in order to purchase what you want.

?

1. **How did rationing work during World War II in the United States?**

2. **A useful technique to help analyze arguments is to construct a parallel argument: Give some examples of this technique.**

3. **Is it "unfair" to allow prices to be bid up to the market price?**

HAVE WE PAINTED OURSELVES INTO A CORNER?

As you will long since have gathered, I support the free market and, as such, oppose price controls. But what am I now to do? It appears that our point against price controls—they lead to shortages—does not of itself suffice. Must opposition to price controls be classed as simply an arbitrary value judgment?

One might in response elaborate a political philosophy showing that the judgment is not arbitrary. Fortunately, we do not have to follow this complicated path here.

1.   **Read Murray Rothbard's, *Ethics of Liberty* (New York: New York University Press, 1998). How would the rights framework elaborated in that book handle the morality of price controls?**

LUDWIG VON MISES TO THE RESCUE

Ludwig von Mises discovered a way out. As he noted, those who complain that prices are "too high" do not think that shortages are a suitable "price" to pay for lower prices. They contend that prices can be lowered without shortages.

And here economic theory shows them mistaken. Thus, we can say that price controls, from the point of view of its own supporters, fails to achieve its goals. It is thus irrational.

Ludwig von Mises
1881–1973

?

1. How does Mises's argument apply to rationing? (Hint: rationing is a measure to limit consumption.)

2. Why is it a strong argument against a view that it cannot secure the aims of its advocates?

Minimum Wages and Wage Control

Chapter 7
Minimum Wages and Wage Control

This chapter is really unnecessary. If you studied the previous chapter on "Price Controls" carefully, this chapter will hold few surprises for you. But wages are such a "hot" topic that an extended treatment of the subject is needed.

With prices, the usual complaint is that they are "too high." With wages the case is different. They are "too low": the rich get richer and the poor get poorer. You have no doubt heard of the alleged "income gap." Is this a real problem? As we shall see, you have already learned enough to assess the economic impact of interference in wage bargains by the government.

1.   **Before reading the rest of this chapter, try to analyze the effect of minimum wage legislation. (Hint: does the fact that we are dealing with a price floor—wages cannot go below a certain amount—rather than a price ceiling change the basic points of our analysis?)**

A DIGRESSION ON EQUALITY

This is an economics textbook, not a philosophy treatise—much as I'd like to forget it. But it will help you in your study of economics if you look at an often unexamined philosophical assumption. When people complain about the gap between the rich and the poor, they take for granted that the ideal state of affairs is equality. We can't have absolute equality, most people concede, but we should get as close to it as we can without sacrificing too much in productivity. Arthur Okun, a leading leftist economist, speaks of an "equality-efficiency tradeoff."

1.   Why do people think that there is a tradeoff between equality and efficiency? Why can't we maximize both equality and efficiency?

2.   Have a look at John Rawls's *A Theory of Justice* (Cambridge, Mass.: Belknap Press, 1999). This is the most influential book of twentieth-century political theory. Look up what Rawls says about the "difference principle."

MORE ON EQUALITY

But why is equality taken to be an uncontested good thing? You might think the answer is obvious. Suppose someone is homeless and starving, and a multi-millionaire passes him by "in silent contempt." Isn't this unfair?

1.   *Extra-credit:* Can you apply a technique of argument you have already learned to help you analyze this example?

A POORLY-CHOSEN EXAMPLE

A good philosophy example helps us understand exactly the issue in dispute. A bad example confuses us: it mixes together two or more different points.

Remember, what we are interested in now is the (alleged) value of equality. An example that aims to show that equality is important should concern itself with equality—nothing else.

By this criterion, the example about the millionaire and the beggar doesn't fare very well. Can you see why not? This example illicitly appeals to another moral view we may share—i.e., it is undesirable that people be very badly off.

But even if we share this view, this does not show that equality is a good thing. To see this, we can change the example so that only equality is involved. Consider two people, a millionaire and billionaire. Is there an ethical problem just because the billionaire is immensely more rich than the poor millionaire? If you don't think so, what does this tell us about the importance of equality?

1.   **"There's no use arguing about equality. It's just a subjective value judgment that many people, especially those on the left of center, share." How would you respond?**

2.   **"We don't need to argue for equality. It is a self-evident truth, as a glance at the Declaration of Independence suffices to show. Why do we need to justify equality through some further principle?" Evaluate.**

BACK TO ECONOMICS

What determines wage rates on the free market? A standard joke among economists is that the correct answer to any question about the subject is "demand and supply." (As you can see, economists don't have very good jokes.)

However poor the joke, the answer is perfectly apt. A wage is a price for labor services of a certain kind. (Remember, there is not one wage rate: each type of work has a separate price.)

Suppose that the market price for professional stilt-walkers is $10.00 per hour. (Stilt-walkers don't come steep.) At this rate, all those who want to accept employment at that price can do so; and all those who wish to purchase stilt-walkers' services at that price can do so as well. Demand and supply balance. I hope you're not surprised. What happens if the government enacts a law that forbids stilt-walkers to be employed at less than $12.00 per hour?

1.   What does happen? Can you figure it out?

THE MYSTERY UNVEILED

At the new price of $12.00 per hour, more people than before will want to be stilt-walkers. (Certainly, for $12.00 per hour, I'd become a stilt-walker.) But some employers will no longer want to avail themselves of the stilt-walkers' services.

Which ones? Obviously, those who found the value of stilt-walkers just slightly higher than $10.00. Faced with the requirement that they pay $12.00 per hour, they will no longer find it worth their while to do so. These marginal buyers will bid the stilt-walkers a swift farewell.

What then, is the upshot? At the new price, $12.00 per hour, more workers are willing to work than at the $10.00 per hour price. But fewer employers wish to purchase labor at this price. Supply and demand no longer balance. Put another way, minimum wage laws cause unemployment.

1. *Extra-credit.* Both here and in the previous chapter, we've spoken of "marginal" buyers or sellers. These are people who "just barely" find a transaction worth making at the market price and will be driven out of the market should the price change in a way unfavorable to them. Is the use of this concept consistent with the Austrian claim that preference is ordinal and cannot be measured?

EXCEPTIONS

We can come up with a few exceptional cases in which minimum wage laws do not cause unemployment. Suppose that stilt-walkers earn $10.00 per hour, and the minimum wage is $5.00. It is safe to predict that this minimum wage regulation will have little effect on unemployment.

1. Draw a demand and supply curve for stilt-walkers, with $10.00 as the market wage. Show how a minimum wage of $5.00 will leave price determination untouched.

AN EXCEPTION

Or will it? As you might have already guessed, there's an exception. The market for workers is affected not only by the prevailing wage rate, but by expectations about future wages. If an employer thinks that the market wage for stilt-walkers will soon fall to $3.00, he will make plans accordingly. If the minimum wage interferes with his plans, his demand schedule will alter.

?

1. **Show why the exception isn't really an exception. (Hint: the minimum wage will have an impact on future demand.)**

2. **What about a minimum wage rate so low it has no effect on either present or expected wages?**

THE MINIMUM WAGE RULE

In general, then, we can say: *a minimum wage will either be useless or will cause unemployment.* Once again, there is another exception: the minimum wage "justifies" itself by changing preference schedules so that the minimum wage becomes the market wage. But why should this happen?

ETHICS

No, I can't stay away from philosophy for long; but, as we have already covered the essentials, we can be brief. The minimum wage rule does not by itself suffice to show that minimum wages are bad. It is a descriptive, not a normative claim.

Further, to justify a negative verdict on minimum wage legislation, it is not enough just to add the non-controversial value-judgment, "unemployment is bad." A supporter of minimum wages could claim that the increased wages for some workers outweighs the unemployment of others.

MISES TO THE RESCUE AGAIN

Once more, Ludwig von Mises offers a way out. Advocates of minimum wages do not characteristically claim that the advantages of higher wages for some justify unemployment for others. Rather, they claim that minimum wage legislation will increase wages without causing unemployment. And this economic theory shows to be false. (If this chapter sounds like a repetition of the last chapter, you have learned your lessons well. If it doesn't, please reread the previous chapter.)

?

1.   **"We're talking about human lives here! The economic principles that determine the price of ordinary goods and services don't apply to human labor." Evaluate.**

2.   **Without minimum wages, employers would be free to pay "starvation wages." Evaluate.**

3.   **Why are minimum wages usually quite low? Why not a $20.00 per hour minimum wage?**

THE ZONE OF INDETERMINACY

Some labor economists will say that the foregoing analysis is crude and oversimplified. (They would say that, wouldn't they?) We have assumed that the free market fixes wages at a certain point: above or below this point, there will be either shortage or surplus.

But why assume this? Perhaps wages are fixed by the market in a zone, rather than at a point. Suppose that the market wage of stilt-walkers is $10.00 per hour. A minimum wage now requires that stilt-walkers be paid $12.00 per hour.

Must unemployment result? Not necessarily. Suppose employers demand exactly the same number of stilt-walkers at $12.00 as at $10.00; and workers prove no more likely to practice "nonsense on stilts" than at the higher price. In other words, neither demand nor supply respond very much to small shifts in price. If so, the minimum wage will not cause unemployment.

Supporters of this view have not offered much evidence in its defense. Why assume that the labor market operates differently from other markets? We don't usually talk about zones of indeterminacy in the price of wheat—or, for that matter, of stilts. Why stilt-walkers?

Further, if there is such a zone, why assume that workers will tend to come out at the low end of it? And, if they do, why is this a situation that requires state intervention?

1. **Why does minimum wage legislation hit teenagers and minorities especially hard?**

2. **List various summer jobs that you have had. Would changes in wage rates have led you to change jobs?**

A COMMONLY MISSED POINT

You may be thinking, "as usual, he's making too much fuss over a point that isn't all that important. Perhaps minimum wage laws do cause unemployment. But, after all, most people earn substantially above minimum wage. Aside from teenagers—and they surely don't matter—minimum wages do not have that much impact."

But this objection construes "wages" too narrowly. Your wage is not only the amount of money you get, but your total benefit package. If you have a pension plan, health insurance, paid vacation, etc., these are all part of wages.

Why? Well, when you are considering a job, don't you take these into account? And when an employer offers you a job, he must calculate the cost of all of these benefits.

In many cases, the government requires that employees be offered a certain benefit package. In the most famous instance, employers must contribute certain premium payments toward the employee's Social Security account. These payments should be considered extensions of minimum wage legislation. Practically everyone is affected by them, and by other governmentally mandated benefits.

?

1. **For various jobs, list the components of the "total benefit package."**

2. **Do you think that workers would prefer more choice in their benefit package, rather than have the government mandate what they must have?**

LABOR UNIONS

As usual in this book, government has been the villain. But another sort of pressure can raise wages for some at the expense of others. Suppose Sam Stiltwalker says: "I don't think $10.00 per hour is adequate recompense for my services. I want $25.00." Well, he can say this—it's a free country—but if $10.00 is the market price, he will find few takers.

Imagine, now, that Sam is a little smarter. He organizes a group of his fellow stilt-walkers and tells his employer, "Unless you raise our wages from $10.00 to $25.00 per hour, we will strike."

Sam has been too clever by half. Remember, at the market price, all those who wish to purchase labor can find sellers. Sam and his friends will quickly be replaced. They have priced themselves out of the market.

Sam's only hope lies in coercion. If he can prevent the employer from hiring replacements, he has a much better chance of getting the wages he wants.

Among ways that labor unions try to block replacements are legislation that forbids firing strikers and the use of force against replacements.

1. Read *The Kohler Strike* by Sylvester Petro (Chicago: Henry Regnery, 1961) for an account of labor unions in action.

2. Replacement workers are often called "scabs". In whose interest is this pejorative language?

3. Why do you think labor unions usually support minimum wage legislation?

Chapter 8
Money: Part 1

THE ORIGIN OF MONEY

Much of economics consists of going over what we have already learned before. The principal reason for this is not that this is an excellent way to learn—though that is true enough. Nor is it that I have little new to offer—of that I am not the best judge. Rather, the genius of Austrian economics consists, in large part, in drawing out the implications of simple principles. To do this, one must constantly revert to these principles.

"PAY NO ATTENTION TO THE
MAN BEHIND THE CURTAIN..."

One of the most basic of these principles we have had continued occasion to stress. A trade will take place if it is mutually beneficial to the parties. If I have three apples and two oranges and you have two apples and three oranges, what will happen if we each prefer to change our fruit portfolios? (Aren't you getting tired of apples and oranges? One of the best features of this chapter is that we'll get to talk about something else.)

Suppose I would rather have two apples and three oranges; and, you, conveniently enough, want three apples and two oranges. If you and I exchange one apple for one orange, we shall each be better off. Other things being equal, then, the trade will be made.

So far, so good. But what happens if I want to trade one apple for one orange, but you do not? Selfish pomologist that you are, you refuse to surrender one of your apples. What am I to do?

You might think the problem has an easy solution. Our principle tells us that a trade will take place if it is to the advantage of the parties engaged in it. If you do not want to give up an apple, the trade is not to your advantage. I cannot then claim by the principle that a trade will take place. I appear to be unable to get an apple from you.

1.   "We can't conclude that a trade won't take place either. All that follows is that one can't appeal to this principle to support the claim that a trade will take place." What's wrong with this objection?

2.   What is the difference between a necessary and a sufficient condition?

3.   Can you give a stronger principle of trade than the one mentioned in the text?

MORE ON EXCHANGE

If you have answered the questions at the end of the previous discussion correctly, then you will realize that my quest for an apple seems doomed. Unless you would rather have one more orange and one fewer apple than you now have, you will not be willing to trade.

Do you see why this is a stronger conclusion than our previous result? Before, we showed that the principle justifying trade—you will make a trade if it makes you better off—does not generate support for the exchange I want.

Now we claim that unless both parties are better off, no trade will take place. A trade will take place, *if and only if* both parties expect to benefit from it.

By now, it should be old hat to you to show why this stronger principle is true. Each person chooses the action, of those alternatives available to him, that will maximize his utility. If a trade will not make you better off, then you will not engage in it. If it will (and you have no still better choice available), then you will make the trade.

1. Give examples in which "If a, then b" is true but "b only if a" is false.

2. Give examples in which "b only if a" is true but "if a, then b" is false.

INDIRECT EXCHANGE

But how am I to get my apple? I must have it! I might attempt to ask someone else to trade with me, if you will not. Surely someone in the class will be willing to part with an apple. (Remember the old motto, "An apple a day keeps the textbook writer away.")

But suppose that no one who owns apples is willing to exchange them for oranges. Does it follow that I cannot obtain apples through exchange? Surprisingly, it does not.

What gives us our room to maneuver? Doesn't the principle given in the previous section rule out my getting apples through exchange? Can you find the loophole?

The answer depends on a subtle distinction. From "I cannot obtain apples by exchanging them for oranges" it does not follow that "I cannot obtain apples by exchange." *This is a stronger conclusion than the premise*. What if I can obtain apples by some other type of exchange?

But, once more, how is this possible, given that no one who owns apples will part with them for oranges? Well, suppose that you will trade an apple for a copy of a book—say, Keynes's *General Theory*. (To make this example more realistic, we need to suppose that you would surrender only a rotten apple for this book.)

Now, I have only to obtain a copy of the book and I can have my apple. (Obviously, if I owned the book already, no problem would arise.) Now, we face a new problem: how can I get it?

Fortunately, someone who owns a copy of Keynes's masterwork is willing to part with it in exchange for an orange. (Since it's *my* example, I am free to postulate whatever preferences I want.) Once I obtain the book, I can next offer my copy of the book to you; and at last I shall obtain my coveted apple.

You may object to the solution in this way. In order to trade one orange for one book, I must prefer having the book to the orange. (Why? If you can't answer even after so much repetition, your chances of passing this course are dim.)

But suppose I don't like the book—in point of fact, I don't like the volume in question. Then, doesn't it follow that I won't make the exchange? In that case, I cannot use the proposed solution to get the apple I want. If I had a copy of the book, I could then exchange it with you for one apple; but, given my dislike for the book, it appears that I cannot obtain one by exchange for an orange. I do like oranges.

> **1.** **See whether you can anticipate the next section. What is wrong with the argument just presented?**

INDIRECT EXCHANGE CONTINUED

When I said that I didn't like the book *General Theory*, what did I mean? Basically, I mean that I do not value the book for its own sake. I would not give up an orange to get the book, if I had to keep the book.

And there exactly lies the flaw in the argument presented just before. I don't have to keep the book—I can use it to trade for something else, an apple. If I obtain a copy of *General Theory*, I can get something I do want to keep. Thus, it is false that the book has less value to me than the orange, even though, just looking at the orange and the book by themselves, I would rather have the orange.

If a good can be used to get other goods that I want, its value to me increases. In this way, other people's preferences affect my own. Because you want a copy of *General Theory* and will give an apple to get it, the book becomes more valuable to me than an orange.

> **1.** **How does our analysis relate to the distinction that Adam Smith and David Ricardo made between use-value and exchange-value?**

STILL MORE ON INDIRECT EXCHANGE

You can readily see why exchange of this kind is sometimes called "triangular" instead of a direct exchange like this:

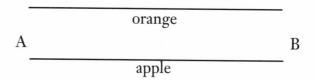

Figure 11. Direct Exchange

We have two exchanges:

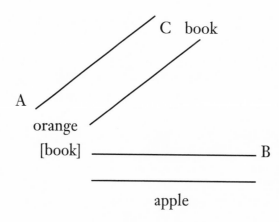

Figure 12. Two Exchanges

(Note that our "triangle" does not require a further exchange between B and C.)

Once given this basic pattern, more and more complicated patterns can be constructed. Suppose no one who has a copy of *General Theory* wants an orange. Perhaps a book owner wants a waffle iron, and I know someone who will exchange a waffle iron for an orange. I first exchange my orange for a waffle iron; next, I exchange the waffle iron for a copy of the book; and, at last, I exchange the book for the apple.

1. **Construct some chains of exchanges. How complicated a series do you think could exist in the real world?**

2. **Consider the first indirect exchange. Can't my devious scheme to obtain an apple be thwarted by the book owner? All he has to do is exchange his book with the apple owner. What is wrong with this objection?**

LIMITS OF INDIRECT EXCHANGE

You can have a lot of fun making up complicated chains of exchanges. (I don't think this is much fun; but, who knows? Maybe you do.) But you can readily see that people who try to use the indirect exchange method to get what they want will encounter difficulties.

What are these? First of all, wherever you take a step in the chain, you must find someone who wants what you then have. This is of course a requirement of all exchanges: it is called the problem of "double coincidence of wants." The more steps in a chain of trade you have to make, the more difficult this problem becomes.

Further, at each step in the chain disaster threatens to strike. Suppose I miscalculate: I think, e.g., that if only I can get a statue of a pink hippopotamus, I can then secure a copy of *General Theory*, enabling me at last to get the apple I want. Unfortunately for me, the owner of *General Theory* shrinks in horror at the statue; and I am stuck with it. Since I would much rather have an orange than the statue, I have lost out on the deal.

But suppose I have calculated all the steps in the chain correctly—textbook authors, after all, are immune from error. Have I then found a good way to get more of what I want? The matter is not so simple.

Even if I line up a series of trades, making no mistakes in doing so, I cannot count the process one of pure gain. Setting up the procedure takes time and effort. This is called "transactions cost". Against the gain I hope to achieve at the end of the process must be set the cost of engaging in it.

1.   **How is the "cost" in "transactions cost" to be assessed?**

2.   **"Since transactions costs are an economic 'bad', our aim, both as individual actors and policymakers, should be to minimize transactions costs." What's wrong with this picture?**

THE PROBLEM OF INDIRECT EXCHANGE COMPOUNDED

To reiterate, there are two main "first-level" problems in indirect exchange: the series of exchanges must be coordinated, and errors may leave you with goods you do not want. Even if you can solve these difficulties, your attempt to do so generates a "second-level" problem: you are confronted with transactions costs.

One way to deal with these problems is to abandon indirect exchange altogether. But then you are limited to what you can get in direct exchange (or, of course, produce yourself). This is obviously a drastic limitation.

The difficulties of indirect exchange suggest a related problem for direct exchange. If you produce something that many people want, e.g., apples, you will probably find it easy to make an exchange.

But what if you produce something few people want? Suppose you are a violin maker, or a writer of economics textbooks. Then, you may have to search far and wide in order to solve the problem of double coincidence of wants. You may have extensive transactions costs even if you engage only in direct exchange.

> 1. **What is the problem of double coincidence of wants? (You should get it right this time.)**
>
> 2. **Given the problem of double coincidence of wants, why do you think people engage in jobs like writing economics textbooks? ("Because they are stupid" is not a good answer.)**

TOWARD A SOLUTION

How do we solve all these problems? You have the material for an answer already to hand. Recall our earlier statement: if you produce goods like apples that many people want, you will find it easy to make an exchange. This should at once suggest a way around all our difficulties.

Suppose you acquire goods that most people want. Then you don't have to worry about complicated chains of trade, and you have reduced transactions costs. Also, if you produce something few people want, you can solve the double coincidence of wants problem by the same means. Once you trade in your ability to write economics textbooks for apples or oranges, your troubles are over.

> **1.**   **Evaluate this objection: "The 'solution' just suggested doesn't work. Of course, if you have goods other people want, you will improve your bargaining position. But why will someone with a good in demand surrender what he has for something few people want? The problem isn't solved at all."**

IS OUR SOLUTION A PSEUDO-SOLUTION?

I hope you didn't make the mistake of failing to read the discussion question above. I cunningly put important points in these sections, as well as questions for review and application. This is one instance where I have done this.

The objection raises two valid concerns. First, someone who trades a good more in demand as an instrument for further trade for one less in demand is, other things being equal, suffering a loss. But it does not follow that no such exchanges will take place. Rather, the person with the good more highly in demand earns a premium. If I want to obtain oranges in return for writing an economics textbook, I shall probably have to be satisfied with getting fewer than I would have obtained had more people been ready to take the use of my skill in exchange for what they want.

The second valid concern raised in the objection is this. Someone who has a good not much in demand for further trade cannot conjure double coincidence of wants out of existence. Even given our solution, he must still find someone who wants what he has for sale. And that person must have a good more in demand for further trade than his own. But if he can overcome this initial hurdle, he is on his way.

HOW A MEDIUM OF EXCHANGE ARISES

A good like oranges thus has two components that determine its value: (1) its use to consumers and producers—people who want to eat oranges, make virtual pets of them, hang them as wall decorations, use them to make juice, etc. and (2) its use as a medium of exchange.

The second use is a bit complicated, and it will be helpful to go over it again. Because oranges are much in demand for further trade, the value of oranges rises. One of the uses of oranges is that people think they can be used to get other things that people want.

What happens if a good gains value because it is thought by most people to be in general demand of this kind? People will then probably expect that in the future, the good will be even more in demand, increasing its value even further.

Let's look at this in more detail.

At the start, *t1*, consumers value oranges for purposes of consumption. Then, at *t2*, consumers who see that many people trade for oranges will value oranges more highly than they otherwise would have done.

Next, at *t3*, consumers who see that even more people than before trade for oranges will tend to value oranges still more highly than before. By this, I mean that they value oranges (1) more highly than they would have without considering the exchange value of oranges at all; and (2) more highly than they would have had they added only the exchange value of oranges at *t1* to their estimation of oranges' value.

If you found the previous paragraph convoluted, imagine how difficult it was to write it! You don't really have to worry about the details. What you do need to remember is the basic principle: *A good that people think will be accepted readily in exchange will gain in value.* Imprint this on your brain.

> **1.   How does the discussion in the previous few pages raise a problem for praxeology? Are all of the steps in the reasoning presented strictly deductive?**

CONVERGENCE

So far, we know that some goods are more heavily in demand for trade than others. Because of this, these goods find their values enhanced.

We can now go further. What happens when market actors see that some goods are more valued than others, in part because of the expectation that they will be highly valued? It seems likely that the goods in the highly valued class (oranges, apples, ice cream) will not be equally in demand for their use in further exchanges. Some will be more valued for this purpose than others.

What will now happen? When people see that some goods are more highly valued than others, their demand as exchange goods will increase. This will be true even if the goods are only slightly more highly valued for exchange than others. If apples are expected to be even more in general demand than oranges, people will want apples rather than oranges.

1. **Evaluate this objection: "What has just been said may be true, but it is not praxeology. According to praxeology, our conclusions have to follow necessarily from the action axiom, the subsidiary postulates, or conclusions drawn from any of these. This has not been accomplished here." Review the chapter on praxeology to help you prepare your answer.**

PRAXEOLOGY AND CONVERGENCE

Contrary to the objection just suggested, the reasoning of our previous section conforms to praxeological law. (A good thing that it does, too, or I would be out of business.) Remember, we are concerned here only with a good's exchange value—its use, as a good believed in general demand, to obtain whatever other goods I want.

Given this fact, even small differences in expected exchange-value count for a great deal. I shall always tend to choose, other things being equal, the good I think likely to have the highest chance of general acceptance by others. Otherwise, I shall not be choosing my highest valued alternative. And we have already shown that I always do choose my highest valued alternative. You will probably find it helpful now to review the discussion of alternatives and choices. (Teachers, please make sure your students act on this suggestion.)

EXTRA-CREDIT SECTION: FURTHER PROBLEMS FOR PRAXEOLOGY

We are not yet out of the woods, as far as praxeology is concerned. How does it follow from the fact that in the indicated circumstances,

I shall always choose the good I expect to have the highest exchange-value, that I shall choose the good that has had in the past the highest exchange-value? And how do we know that goods must have differing exchange-values? These are difficult questions, and in part too advanced for this book.

1.   **Solve the problems just discussed. Then mail the answers to me.**

MONEY AND BANKING

Long before now, you have probably thought this is a strange chapter. It is supposed to be about money and banking; but so far, it seems, we have said nothing about these subjects. As you will see in the following chapter, however, we have taken the essential steps toward understanding this difficult topic.

Chapter 9
Money: Part 2

CONVERGENCE ONCE MORE

In the last chapter, we argued that economic actors in search of a medium of exchange will tend to converge on a few goods. People who want to obtain goods that they think will always be accepted by others will tend to choose the same goods, more or less.

Can we go further? What properties will the goods they select have? Here we take a temporary leave of absence from praxeology and engage in historical inquiry of a sort.

We are asking: what properties does it seem reasonable to want in a medium of exchange? To put the question another way, what will people tend to choose as *money*? We shall define money as *a good almost universally accepted in a market for purposes of exchange*. If you want to exchange what you have produced at all, you will most likely accept money for it.

---

1. Must a good be *universally* accepted to count as money? Suppose someone will accept only a particular spider in exchange for his copy of *General Theory* and not the money to buy the spider he wants. Must we conclude that because of this person, money does not exist in his society?

PROPERTIES OF A MEDIUM OF EXCHANGE

Historically, all sorts of things have served as money, ranging from cattle to sea shells to sugar. In prison camps during World War II, cigarettes were used as money.

But most societies that have allowed a market in money to develop have converged on gold and silver as the commodities used for media of exchange.

First of all, the medium of exchange should be durable. Ice cream, however desirable, would not be a good medium of exchange because it is perishable. True, you can keep it in the freezer; but this is costly. And how would you carry it around to exchange it for other things?

BANKO THE MAGICIAN

Austrian Hundert Schilling

This leads to a related property that money is likely to have. It should be readily divisible into small units. Can you see why elephants would not be a good choice as money? Suppose you want to buy a candy bar. How could you do so, if one elephant were the smallest unit of currency? Gold and silver, by contrast, can easily be cut into small units. (In countries on a gold or silver standard, metals of less value, such as nickel or copper, are often used for the smallest denominations of coin.)

The third quality follows from our discussion in the previous chapter. The medium of exchange must have qualities that make it widely acceptable. The beauty of gold and silver has made these metals widely desirable in a great many societies.

To sum up, with a free market, we may expect gold or silver (or both) to be adopted as the medium of exchange.

1.   **Give examples of different commodities that have been adopted as money by various societies.**

2.   **Why do you think that many writers have criticized the desire to amass gold? (Murray N. Rothbard and Dr. Joseph Salerno have termed this phenomenon "aureophobia.")**

MONEY AS A STORE OF VALUE

We have now completed our first historical excursion. We shall assume that a society has adopted gold as its medium of exchange; and, proceeding by praxeological reasoning, ask what follows from this fact.

One advantage of a gold (or silver) standard follows at once from one of its physical properties. Because gold is *durable*, people who own it need not make their exchanges all at once. If I own gold, I can save it until I find something that I want to buy with it.

As we have seen already, a medium of exchange extends our ability to obtain different goods. If I wish to trade economic textbooks for ice cream (I'm sick of apples), I must find an ice-cream owner who wants a textbook. If I have gold, I have the much easier task of finding an ice-cream owner who wants gold. And of course the task is much easier in large part because *he* wants the gold so that he can buy the things he wants. (Have I repeated this idea enough times yet?)

Now we see that the gold not only extends the *space* of goods available to me. It also extends the time in which I can purchase them. In doing so gold acts as a store of value: this is one of the main functions of money.

?

1.   *Extra-credit:* **By extending the time in which someone can purchase goods, how does gold also extend the space of goods available? Notice that "time" is used literally here but "space" figuratively.**

MONEY'S EFFECT ON OTHER GOODS

As always, let's review. We started with direct exchange: I trade one orange for one apple. From this we moved to indirect exchange. Since you don't want my orange but do want a copy of *General Theory*, I trade my orange for the book and then trade the book for the apple. Goods in general demand for further trade, we saw, will have their value enhanced by their being perceived to be in wide demand. People in a market society will tend to converge on one or two goods, almost always gold or silver, as the medium of exchange.

Now we must attend to a rather more subtle point, often overlooked. Remember, that *before* gold was adopted as the medium of exchange in our model market, we had several goods, e.g., oranges, whose value increased because of their being perceived to be in general demand. People wanted oranges, among other goods, in part because they thought that other people would take oranges in trade.

The question that now arises is this. Once gold has become the generally accepted medium of exchange, what happens to the part of the value of oranges that rested on oranges' exchange value?

Before you try to answer, let's make sure that you understand the question. Before gold became accepted as money, oranges increased in value because people wished to use *them* as a medium of exchange. Once gold is accepted, what happens to this part of the value of oranges?

Fairly obviously, it decreases; depending on circumstances, it may lose this part of its value altogether. People who want to exchange what they produce for a good that will be generally acceptable to others will now want gold, not oranges. Once a good is adopted as the medium of exchange, it becomes the main good whose value is determined by its general acceptability.

1. **If gold is the medium of exchange, will the component of oranges' value that depends on its general acceptability always fall to zero? Can you think of circumstances in which it will not?**

THE MONEY REGRESSION THEOREM

I fear I must now issue a warning. The following section is among the most difficult in the book. It cannot be consigned to the limbo of extra-credit because it deals with one of the key theorems of economics.

Money, as we have explained, did not arise through the command of the state. Neither did it arise through an explicit agreement. People did not say: "From this day forward, commodity x shall be the medium of exchange."

Rather, money arose through the spontaneous processes of the market. First, gold was valued as a consumption good. It is mainly used for jewelry but can also be employed in other areas. For example, it can be used to fill teeth, or for certain special industrial processes, etc.

Next, gold gained value because people thought it would be generally accepted in exchange. And when people saw that it had this property to a greater extent than other goods, people valued it for exchange purposes even more than before. Thus gold became money.

A few points about money need special stress. These are not especially difficult to grasp, but theorists outside the Austrian camp often ignore them. To begin with, the value of gold is due almost wholly to its services as a medium of exchange. *But gold did not begin as a medium of exchange.* It began as an ordinary commodity, with utility for purpose other than exchange.

Carl Menger, the founder of the Austrian School of Economics, pioneered this account of the origin of money in his *Principles of Economics*. In so doing, he achieved a crucial breakthrough in economic theory. Before him, people often thought that money arose by an explicit agreement to accept a given substance as money. John Locke, a great political theorist but a not-so-great economist, held this view. Menger showed that Locke and those who thought as he did were in this instance wrong.

1. See if you can find out the origin of the phrase "the result of human action but not of human design."

2. "Once again, praxeology has been abandoned. Menger's analysis is simply a historical account. There is nothing necessary about it." Discuss this objection.

3. Do a report on F.A. Hayek's work on spontaneous order. Suggested reading: Hayek's 3 volume work, *Law, Legislation & Liberty* (Chicago: University of Chicago Press, 1978).

MISES ON MONEY REGRESSION

I have so far failed to fulfill a promise; and you are probably glad. The material on money regression was supposed to be hard, but so far (I hope) it hasn't been. Now the fun begins.

How does the market determine the value of an ordinary commodity, e.g., ice cream? As you will recall from previous chapters, those magic words demand and supply answer the question. And what, in turn, determines demand and supply? The preferences of the demanders and suppliers of ice cream.

Money, on Menger's account, is a commodity; so the same analysis should apply to it. The value of gold, then, depends on the demand and supply of gold. The demand and supply schedules, further, rest on the utilities of the demanders and suppliers of gold.

AT LAST WE GET TO MISES

So far, so good. But now a problem looms. The demand for gold depends on the utility of gold. But what determines this? Remember, the utility of gold resides almost entirely in its use as a medium of exchange. *People want gold because they can use it to get whatever else they want.*

Can you see why this poses a problem? We are attempting to determine the value, i.e., the utility of gold. But the utility of gold depends on its *purchasing-power*, its value in obtaining other goods. We appear to be engaged in circular reasoning. That is, we are explaining something in terms of itself. And this is a major logical no-no.

1. **Give examples of circular reasoning.**

2. **Is circular reasoning always wrong? Aren't some statements self-explanatory?**

It appears then that money is the great exception in value theory. We cannot use conventional utility theory to explain the value of gold, since the utility of gold depends on the value of gold. Hence we must look elsewhere. (I warned you this was tough!)

Ludwig von Mises showed in *The Theory of Money and Credit* (1912) that the value of money can be accounted for by ordinary utility theory. The attempt to do so need not involve reasoning in a circle.

How did Mises find a way out of the circle? He noted that the value of money today depends on the value of money yesterday. When people are trying to value gold, they must estimate the purchasing power of gold. Their only basis for doing so is the value of money yesterday.

Note that Mises did not mean that the value of money today equals its value yesterday. If that were his contention, Mises's theory would be false. It would have the consequence that the value of money never changes (can you see why?), which is contrary to obvious fact. Mises is saying that people must use the value of money yesterday as the basis for estimating its value today.

1. *Extra-credit:* In an extra-credit section in the previous chapter, I raised a problem that involved praxeology. People will tend to converge on one or two goods as a medium of exchange. In doing so, they choose the good they think most likely to have the highest exchange value. The problem raised was this: is it necessarily true that their estimates depend on which item has been most valued as an instrument of exchange? Mises's analysis of the value of money appears to solve this difficulty.

HAS MISES SOLVED HIS PROBLEM?

It appears that he has not really done so. True, he has avoided the circle: He does not explain the value of money by the value of money. He explains the value of money today by its value yesterday.

But is this really an improvement? What explains the value of money yesterday? Obviously, the value of money on the day before yesterday. And the value of that? Its value on the day before that, and so on. We appear to have exchanged a circle for a regress. In a regress, we say: A depends on B, B depends on C, C depends on D . . . and we never reach a term that is not dependent on some previous term. Although this can be disputed, it seems that a fully satisfactory explanation cannot take this form.

Here precisely lies Mises's genius as a monetary theorist. He showed that his account of the value of money by its value on the previous day does not entail an unsatisfactory regress. What happens when we keep pushing back the explanation? The value of gold at *t* depends on its value at *t-1*, which depends on its value at *t-2* . . . Eventually, we reach a day in which gold had no value as an instrument for obtaining other commodities. The purchasing power component of its value drops out, and the value of gold on "day one" depends entirely on its use for non-monetary purposes.

Mises thus integrated the explanation of money's value into general utility theory. Money is not an exception: its value can be explained by the same theory as other commodities. The purchasing power of money just makes the explanation rather more complicated.

Do you see a crucial premise needed if Mises's explanation is to work? There must be a day one in which the monetary commodity's value is not determined at all by estimates of its purchasing power. Otherwise, we shall not have escaped the regress. Of course gold, the example I used to explain Mises's argument, does have a non-purchasing power value. But Mises does not contend that gold (or silver) must be adopted as a society's requirement. Nevertheless, money must originate as a non-monetary commodity.

Can you see why it must? Without a value on day one, there would be no means available by which people could estimate the purchasing power of money. And it is essential that they be able to do this in order for money to serve as a medium of exchange.

An assortment of paper money

To Mises's argument there is an obvious objection. What about paper money? Some paper money is merely a claim receipt for gold, but other paper money is not. This type of money, called *fiat money*, is simply declared to be money by the government. Absent this declaration, its value would be nil. The fiat money would then just be worthless pieces of paper.

Regardless of whether the government should issue fiat money (a question we shall address in the next chapter), it very often does so. Is this not a refutation of Mises's account? He says that money *must* originate as a commodity. But fiat money does not so originate. Hence Mises's theory collapses; "A beautiful theory, ruined by a stubborn fact."

In fact, Mises's theory does not have the consequences our supposed refutation imputes to it. Mises does *not* deny the possibility of fiat money. Rather, he claims that fiat money is parasitic on commodity money. In the absence of commodity money, people would have no way to estimate the purchasing power of fiat money, and this sort of money could not exist.

?

1. Why does the existence of money require that people be able to estimate its purchasing power?

2. "Mises gives an account of the value of money, but he does not show that any competing account is impossible. Hence he does *not* show that money must originate as a commodity." Evaluate this objection.

The Gold Standard

10

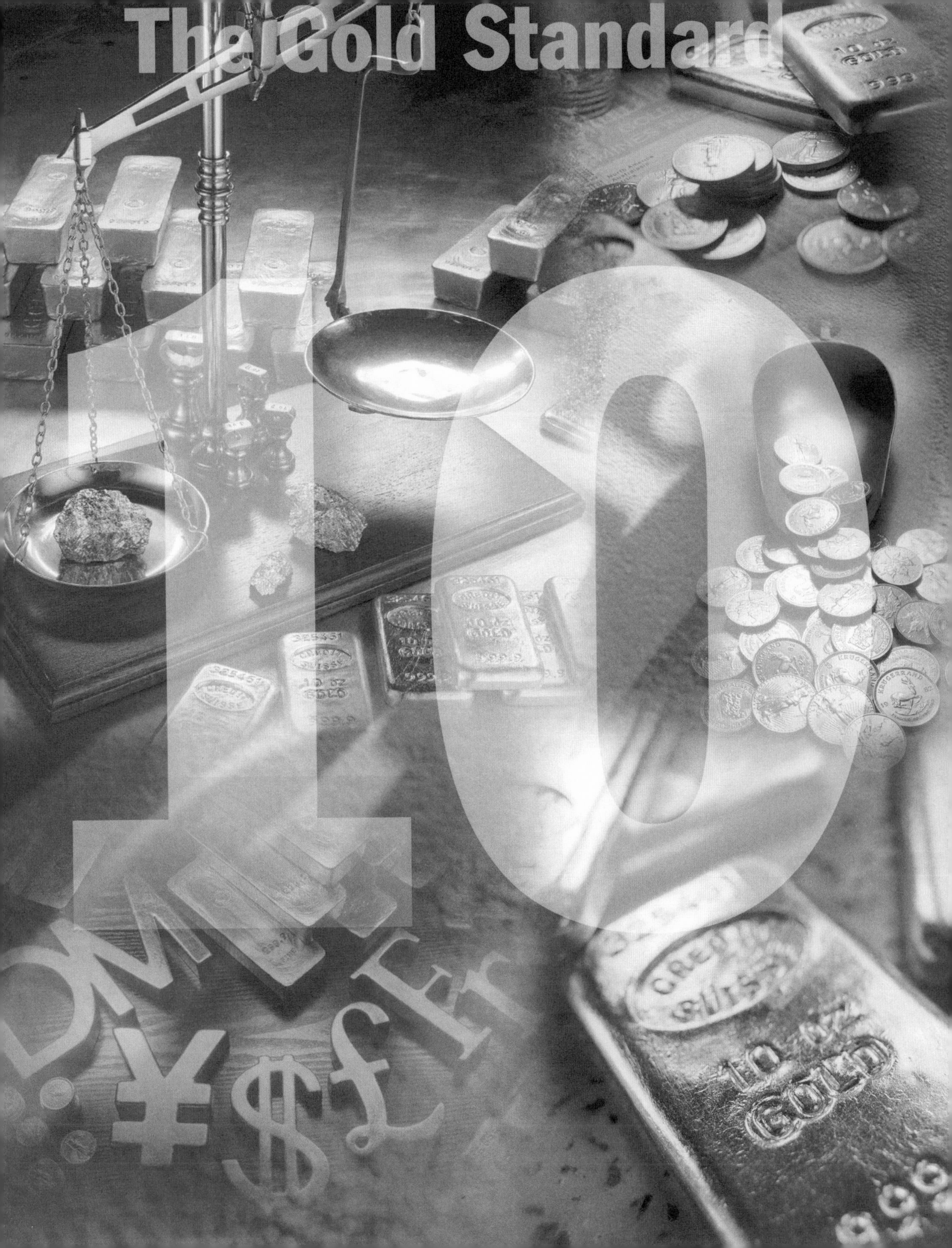

Chapter 10
The Gold Standard

Money, we have seen, begins as a commodity—otherwise people would not know what value to give it. But, what commodity? As mentioned in the previous chapter, this is not something we can determine by *a priori* reasoning. Many different goods have served as money—including cows and cigarettes.

But, I am sure you will recall, although we cannot figure out which good a society must adopt as money, we can establish some general principles that narrow the range of choice. A good can become money only if it is widely accepted by people in a society. Further, people must believe that it will be accepted if offered in exchange.

1. Why is the latter requirement needed? Why isn't it enough if the members of a society accept a good in exchange? Why must people also believe that it will be accepted?

2. It's easy to understand how a society could adopt cows as money: think of an agricultural community where cows feature prominently. But how can cigarettes get to be money?

AN UNUSUAL CHOICE

The group that chose cigarettes was in an extraordinary situation. It consisted of soldiers in a prisoner of war camp. Since everyone realized that (nearly) everyone else wanted cigarettes, then, no doubt to the dismay of the American Medical Association, cigarettes were a highly demanded good. They became money in the way the money regression theorem indicates.

1.   **"Doesn't the cigarette example really disprove the regression theorem? Didn't people in the camp agree among themselves that cigarettes would be considered money? But the regression theorem says money isn't established by agreement." What is wrong with this objection? Hint: does it follow from the theorem that the evolution of money must take place slowly?**

THE USUAL CHOICE

Were you able to figure out the answer to the last question? Remember, the regression theorem says that the value of the money commodity cannot be determined just by decision. But if people know that cigarettes will be generally accepted, and are aware, through trades, of the price of other goods in terms of cigarettes, things can move very fast.

In most societies, cigarettes are not the medium of exchange. As mentioned before we digressed onto cigarettes, there are some general principles that limit the range of goods that will be chosen as money. These principles, as you will recall from the previous chapter, have led most societies with access to gold or silver to adopt one of these metals, or both, as money.

1.   **Review the properties of money that make gold and silver desirable mediums of exchange.**

2.   If gold and silver are in fact so useful as money, why isn't the United States on the gold standard?

Sometimes, a society will use both gold and silver as money. Usually, silver will be used for smaller transactions, gold for larger. A monetary system with two metals at once poses a problem. We will have some prices of goods given in gold and others given in silver.

1.   How may these prices be compared with each other?

2.   *Extra-credit:* Why does the answer to the first problem suggest a further problem about the prices of other goods? How can this difficulty be resolved?

THE MARKET SOLUTION

The key to our first problem is straightforward. Gold and silver are commodities, just like apples and oranges. They can then trade against each other. For example, the market may establish this price: 1 ounce of gold exchanges for 16 ounces of silver. Suppose this ratio is chosen, will it always remain constant? That is, will gold and silver always exchange according to the formula just given?

As I hope you have realized, the answer is no. The ratio is a price; and just like other prices, it is determined by demand and supply. These, in turn, depend on the utilities of the buyers and seller. (Go back to the chapters on utility and demand and supply for a

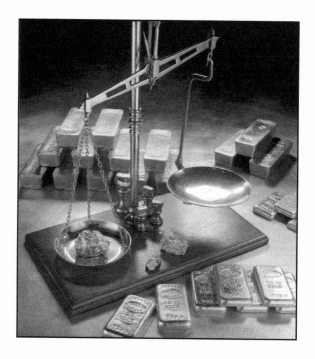

review. You cannot go over these basic principles too many times. To understand economics, you must know demand and supply.)

Let's assume that more silver is mined while the amount of gold stays the same. As more silver enters the market, the marginal utility of silver decreases. (Why?) What will be the effect on the exchange ratio of gold and silver?

People will now have to give up more silver than before to get an ounce of gold. We will have a new ratio of exchange, e.g., 1 ounce of gold exchanges for 16.5 ounces of silver.

1.   **Draw supply and demand diagrams to illustrate the change just described. (Of course, I could have put them in the book! But it's much better that you, the student, construct them for yourself. Besides, it's easier for me.)**

2. Draw supply and demand diagrams showing the effect of an increase in the supply of both metals; a decrease in both; and an increase in one accompanied by a decrease in the supply of the other. I really make you work, don't I?

OTHER GOODS

The market has established an exchange ratio, say 16 to 1, between ounces of silver and gold. Is everything now all right?

No, not necessarily. Some goods will be priced in gold and others in silver. These prices, of course, will be determined by the demand and supply of these goods, relative to the demand and supply of gold and silver, respectively. For example, 1000 oranges may exchange for ½ ounce of silver.

1. What do you think the gold price of 1000 oranges would be, given the silver price just quoted?

OTHER GOODS CONTINUED

In the market, we will have all sorts of different exchange ratios, or prices, some stated in terms of gold, some in terms of silver. All these prices must "match" the gold–silver exchange ratio.

What does this mean? Suppose someone wants to buy oranges but doesn't have any silver. He asks the orange grower, "How much gold must I give you for your 1000 oranges?" (Speakers in economics textbooks often express themselves in stilted sentences.) Our Orangeman is no dummy; he replies, "⅛ ounce of gold." The owner of gold, eager to secure the oranges, accepts. Can you see the problem that now arises? We have the following exchange ratios:

16 ounces of silver exchanges for 1 ounce of gold

½ ounce of silver exchanges for 1000 oranges

⅛ ounce of gold exchanges for 1000 oranges

As Lord Tennyson the great British poet, says, in "The Charge of the Light Brigade," "Someone had blundered." You should easily discern who it is: it's the sap who gave up ⅛ ounce of gold to get 1000 oranges.

The fortunate Orangeman now has ⅛ ounce of gold. We can now obtain 2 ounces of silver for his gold. (Why?) After doing so, he can buy 4000 oranges. (If he is even more lucky, he can start the round again, this time getting ½ ounce of gold from the sap for 4000 oranges.)

Unfortunately for the Orangeman, but fortunately for the sap, this situation will soon come to an end. Other Orangemen will attempt to get in on the good deal. They want the gold for themselves: they will not act as United Orangemen. But the sap has only a limited amount of gold to offer for oranges. How can each Orangeman get as much as possible for himself? He will offer the sap a better deal. He will, say, offer 2000 oranges for ⅛ ounce of gold.

?

> **1.   Why will he do so? The sap will give up 1/8 ounce of gold for 1000 oranges. Why offer an extra 1000?**

THE SAP GETS WISE

If he didn't offer more oranges, what would happen? He might be shut out of the market. His fellow Orangemen would all be trying to get the gold; and there is not enough to go around. If he offers 2000 oranges, his chances to get gold increase. The sap prefers to get 2000 oranges rather than 1000 oranges for his ⅛ ounce of gold. (He isn't that idiotic.) The Orangeman will make less profit than before, but it is still well worth it for him to up his offer.

1. **Work through the exchange ratios to show why it is still to the advantage of the Orangeman to get 1/8 ounce of gold for 2000 oranges. How high do you think the bidding will go?**

2. **What do you think the sap will do when he sees Orangemen bidding up the price?**

THE SAP GETS WISE, PART 2

More and more Orangemen will see the opportunity to make a killing in the market. And perhaps others, who do not now own oranges, will see the advantage to be gained by purchasing them. Once they have the oranges in hand, they can attempt to secure gold from the sap.

Meanwhile, the sap sees that his gold is in demand. (Even idiocy is usually not of infinite extent.) He will suspect that he has been offering too much gold and will lower his offer.

Thus, our exchange ratio of ⅛ ounce gold for 1000 oranges faces pressure on two fronts. Orangemen offer more oranges and the sap offers fewer ounces of gold. How long will this go on? Until no profits from a series of trades can be obtained. Gains from a series of trades, based on price discrepancies, are called arbitrage gains. We considered them in an earlier chapter, where we discussed the law of one price. Here we see that there is nothing special about money. Gold and silver, just as much as oranges and apples, obey the law of one price.

> **1.   If gold and silver behave like regular commodities, why do you think that many people regard money as subject to completely different economic laws from other goods?**

ENTER THE STATE

Suppose, once more, that silver and gold exchange at a 16 to 1 ratio. In the way I have just explained, all prices of goods on the market "match": no gains are to be had from arbitrage transactions.

"All well and good," certain economic reformers will say, "but the balance is easily upset. As soon as the quantity of gold or silver changes, the ratio of 16 to 1 is outdated and must be altered. But it takes time to do so. Meanwhile, the possibility of arbitrage is present. Why not make calculation of prices easier? To do so, let us make the 16 to 1 ratio permanent. Then, we never have to worry about arbitrage in money again."

> **1.   What ethical assumptions about arbitrage and calculation does our imagined reformer make? Are these assumptions justifiable?**

DIGRESSION ON ETHICS

One of the themes of this book emerges here with crystal clarity. It is very easy to assume that certain ethical views, or "value judgments" should be adopted, even though examination shows them to be controversial and in need of justification.

Our reformer has made two such controversial assumptions. First, he correctly notes that changes in supply and demand take time before they affect prices. Even though the 16 to 1 ratio no longer corresponds to the actors' present utilities, it remains in place until changed.

But why should we think that something is wrong with this? Why should adjustment of prices to changes in demand and supply be instantaneous, or at any rate, faster than the market accomplishes by itself? Be careful not to make an unjustified assumption about what I am saying here. We do not contend that the ideal of instantaneous price adjustments is misplaced.

Rather, I wish all readers to note that an ethical assumption has been made by the reformer. If he moves from (1) price adjustment takes time; to (2) price adjustment takes too much time, he has taken a step that requires argument in its support.

And our reformer has smuggled in another unexamined assumption: adjustments that take place through arbitrage are "bad." What is wrong with arbitrage? Our reformer must tell us. Once more, we have not assumed that arbitrage is morally all right; we have wished merely to call attention to a burden of proof too often overlooked.

1.   **Give other examples in which proposals for economic reform contain smuggled-in value judgments.**

GRESHAM'S LAW

We shall not, for the moment, take our discussion of ethics further. Here we shall restrict ourselves to "positive" economics. (Recall the distinction between positive and normative statements, discussed earlier.)

Suppose, once again, that the market has established the 16 to 1 ratio. New gold mines in Patagonia are discovered, and an increased quantity of gold has come onto the market. Assuming that utilities otherwise remain unchanged, the price of gold will fall. One ounce of gold will be able to command only 15 ounces of silver in exchange, for example.

But the state has imposed a 16 to 1 ratio. If you have one ounce of gold, you will be able to get 16 ounces of silver for it in the market. You would have been willing, by hypothesis, to take 15 ounces of silver for your gold; but you certainly have no objections to getting an extra ounce.

Silver dealers will prove more recalcitrant. The 16 to 1 ratio no longer reflects the market price. If it is enforced, silver dealers will be less willing than before to offer silver on the market. Gold will tend to become the exclusive medium of exchange.

Why will these results ensue? We must, as always, revert to a basic principle. Money is a commodity.

> **?**
>
> 1.   **How does this principle enable us to analyze the effects of a fixed exchange ratio?**

SURPLUSES AND SHORTAGES

We hope that you answered the question by reference to surpluses and shortages. Remember the effect of a maximum price below the market price? There will be a greater quantity of the good demanded at the artificially lower price than will be offered for sale. In brief, there will be a shortage. This is exactly what has happened in our example. The price of silver is artificially low. Its market value is 1/15 ounce of gold, but its state-mandated price is only 1/16 ounce of gold. Hence a shortage.

Looked at from the opposite angle, the price of gold is artificially high. There is a surplus of gold at the artificially enforced ratio. Purchasers of gold demand a lesser quantity of gold at the 16 to 1 ratio than suppliers offer at that price.

In sum, money overvalued by the state will tend to drive money under valued by the state off the market. This is Gresham's Law, usually stated as "bad money drives out good." Our formulation, which comes from Murray Rothbard, is preferable to the traditional one. It tells us what "bad" and "good" money are.

A SINGLE METAL STANDARD

As we have learned in this chapter, the free market can readily handle a system with both gold and silver as money. So long as the state does not impose price controls, both metals will circulate as money.

But people's preferences may change. They may find two sorts of money, with frequently fluctuating exchange ratios, to be inconvenient. In that case the market stands ready with a solution. If enough people stop using one of the metals as money, it will cease to be money. Remember the money regression theorem? The demonetization process goes exactly in reverse from the path it delineates.

A commodity that grows more and more in demand as a medium of exchange gains extra value by this fact. Silver, e.g., becomes valuable not only for its use in rings or teeth, but for its services in making exchange easier.

If some people stop accepting silver in exchange, then it will lose its value as a medium of exchange. As it loses value, it becomes even less demanded by market exchangers. A spiral-like effect occurs, just the opposite of the process by which money is created.

If a commodity loses all (or nearly all) of its value as a medium of exchange, it has been demonetized. Its value is now determined just like that of any other non-monetary good. Though this is not a praxeological law, it is safe to predict that a free market will tend to supplant a two-metals currency with a single-metal standard, for convenience. The metal chosen will normally be gold.

1.   Why will a free market tend to establish a gold rather than a silver standard?

Conclusion

In this book, we have tried to convey one fundamental lesson. It is possible to think in a systematic, logical way about economics. You need not accept statements just because "the book says so," and you do not have to wait until graduate school to find out the basis for what you are asked to believe.

To understand economics requires only careful attention to reasoning, in some cases perhaps a little difficult and abstract. (I didn't mention this feature at the start, in order not to scare anyone off.) At least, this is the case if the economics in question is Austrian economics, the type we have endeavored to present to you.

In it, we begin with the action axiom and deduce from it powerful theorems, such as the law of diminishing marginal utility concentrated on the application of Austrian reasoning to two key areas, price and the nature of money.

What is the law of demand? What is wrong with Marx's labor theory of value? Why must money originate from a non-monetary commodity? These are a few of the questions you should now be able to answer, if you have made it through my bad jokes.

Further, I hope you will now realize how prices coordinate demand and supply without government interference. Measures of intervention, such as price and wage controls, fail to achieve the purposes their advocates profess. In like manner, the government cannot originate money by *fiat*, out of thin air.

Of course, if you conclude from this that government "should" not intervene, you have made a normative judgment. I hope that you now understand how judgments of value differ from descriptive statements, as well as how knowledge of matters of fact help us make informed policy decisions.

If you have studied this book carefully, you should be ready to read for yourselves such great Austrian economists as Carl Menger, Eugen von Böhm-Bawerk, Ludwig von Mises, and Murray N. Rothbard. I am well content to be, as John Locke said in another context, their underlaborer.

Glossary

Arbitrage: gains that come from taking advantage of differences in prices in local markets. Arbitrageurs see these differences and bring about a single price for each good.

Arbitrageurs: those who take advantage of price discrepancies in the market for a good.

Austrian Economics: a type of economics based upon deduction from the nature of human action, especially stressing the subjective nature of value.

Austrian School: a group of economists including Menger, Böhm-Bawerk, Mises, and Rothbard, whose work is based on the subjective theory of value.

Axiom: a foundational principle, taken to be evident and not in need of derivation.

Barter: exchange of goods not involving money.

Capital: (1) goods used in production. These goods are not valued for the immediate satisfactions they provide, but for their help in transforming goods into finished products.

(2) the monetary value of goods just described. Warning: Do not confuse these two senses.

Capitalism: an economic system characterized by private ownership of the means of production.

Categorical syllogism: a deductive argument of certain type (see **syllogism**), all the premises of which are assertions.

Commodities: goods bought and sold on the market.

Communism: a synonym for socialism, usually of a radical kind.

Cost: the utility of the highest valued alternative not chosen.

Cost of production: the value of the highest alternative foregone in order to produce something.

Deduction: the process of reasoning from premises to a conclusion, in accord with the laws of logic.

Deduction: a type of reasoning which draws conclusions from premises.

Deflation: a decrease in the supply of money in an economic system.

Demand: in economics, the amount of one good offered to purchase another good. Not the bare desire for a good, as often used in ordinary English.

Demand and supply: the basic determinants of price. **Demand** is the quantity of goods consumers are willing to offer for a particular quantity of a commodity. **Supply** is the quantity of the commodity sellers are willing to offer at a given price.

Demand schedule: a table of the quantity of a good consumers wish to buy at various prices.

Diminishing marginal utility, law of: a basic principle of praxeology, according to which the supply of a good is devoted to increasingly less-valued uses.

Double coincidence of wants: a necessary condition for exchange. Each exchanger must prefer what the other offers to what he already has.

Equality: the assumption that goods exchanged are in some sense identical.

Equilibrium: a situation in which buyers and sellers can make no mutually beneficial exchanges.

Ethical assumption: a statement that something morally ought to be the case.

Exchange: the trade of one economic good for another.

Exchange ratios: statements of what quantity of any good will exchange for what quantity of another, e.g., if one apple exchanges for one orange, then apples and oranges are in a 1:1 exchange ratio.

Exchange-value: the worth of an economic good in trade.

Expectations: assumptions about future economic conditions, especially prices.

Fiat money: money issued by the state, without any commodity backing.

Fixed costs: costs that, at the time an economic decision is made, have already been expended.

Fluctuating exchange ratios: exchange ratios, especially of money, which are determined by the market and hence vary.

Frational reserve banking: a system in which a bank can issue multiple receipts for the monetary commodity it has on hand.

Gold standard: a monetary system in which gold is the generally accepted monetary commodity.

Gresham's Law: the principle that money overvalued by the state will tend to drive out money undervalued by the state.

Hedonism: an ethical system that ranks choices by the amount of pleasurable sensations to which they give rise.

Hermeneutician: someone who uses or advocates hermeneutics.

Hermeneutics: a view that human action cannot be understood by scientific laws, but must be grasped in an act of intuitive apprehension.

Historicism: the doctrine that there are no universally valid economic laws. Economic principles apply, at most, to particular historical periods.

Hypothesis: an assumption, usually in the form "if A, then B."

If-clause: the part of a hypothetical that states a certain condition.

Imputation: the process by which the value of consumer goods is transferred backward to the goods that produce them.

Indirect exchange: trade that does not secure the commodity desired in a single exchange, but proceeds by one or more intermediate steps.

Inflation: an increase in the supply of money in an economic system.

Interest rate: the premium that must be paid to obtain the use of money or capital. Principally determined by the rate of time preference.

Intransitive preferences: preferences of the form: A is preferred to B; B is preferred to C; but it is not the case that A is preferred to C.

Labor: human expenditure of effort in production.

Law of marginal utility: the principle that the units of a good will be directed to satisfy the highest ranking preferences not yet satisfied.

Law of one price: the tendency for a uniform price for a given commodity to prevail on the market.

Labor theory of value: the view that the value of a good is the labor time required to make it.

Logic: the normative science of reasoning.

Marginal buyers: buyers who, at a slightly higher price than the market price, would exit the market.

Marginal unit: the unit of a good devoted to the lowest ranked preference of the preferences that the good satisfies.

Marginal utility: the value of the last unit of a commodity. Alternatively, the value of a unit or a good, if one unit of the good had to be given up.

Market: the setting in which economic exchanges take place.

Market clearing price: the price at which the quantity of a good demanded equals the quantity supplied.

Marxism: a system of economics devised by Karl Marx (1818–1883) based on the labor theory of value. It calls for the replacement of capitalism with socialism.

Medium of exchange: a good used to facilitate the exchange of other goods.

Minimum wage legislation: a law forbidding the offer of employment at a wage below a specified rate.

Money: a commodity whose principal use is to facilitate the exchange of other commodities. It is demanded because each person knows that others will accept it in exchange.

Money regression theorem: an argument, developed by Menger and Mises, that the purchasing power of money must originate from the use of the money commodity as a non-monetary good.

Neoclassical economics: a type of economics that makes extensive use of equilibrium assumptions, is heavily mathematical, and is incompletely subjectivist.

One-hundred percent reserve banking: a banking system in which all money certificates must be fully backed by the monetary commodity.

Ought-statement: a statement of what should be the case, as opposed to what is the case.

Pareto optimal situation: a state of affairs in which no person in society can have his utility increased by redistribution of resources without making someone else worse off.

Praxeology: a deductive science that examines the implications of the axiom that human beings act.

Preference: a ranking of available alternatives: if S chooses A over B, then S *prefers* A to B.

Premises: statements from which conclusions are drawn.

Price: the ratio of exchange between two commodities.

Price ceiling: a legally imposed maximum price.

Price controls: forcible interference, usually by the state, with market prices determined by supply and demand.

Price determination: the process by which the price of a commodity in a market is fixed.

Purchasing power of money: the amount of commodities a unit of money is able to buy.

Rationing: a system for distributing goods when demand exceeds supply under a governmentally mandated price.

Reductio: a proof that shows that denial of the desired conclusion leads to a contradiction.

Regression theorem: the principle that the value of money ultimately stems from the money commodity's nonmonetary use.

Rent: the price paid for the use of an asset that belongs to someone else.

Scientific socialism: a synonym for Marxism, based on a Marxist belief that the onset of socialism is probably inevitable.

Shortage: a situation in which the quantity of a good demanded exceeds the quantity supplied.

Social Security: a governmentally mandated system in which workers and employees are taxed and retired workers receive a pension. Not equivalent to a private insurance plan.

Socialism: a system of production based on central ownership of the means of production.

Spontaneous processes: a series of events that generates an organized outcome without central direction.

Strike: an organized work stoppage, aimed at inducing an employer to offer better conditions of work.

Subjective theory of value: the view that economic value is determined by the choices of actors in the market.

Supply: a good offered for sale in the market.

Surplus: a situation in which the quantity of a good supplied exceeds the quantity demanded.

Syllogism: a form of reasoning in which a conclusion is deduced from a major and minor premise.

Symbolic logic: a system of logic not restricted to the subject-predicate statements of ordinary language.

Tautology: a statement, e.g., a definition or part of a definition that is true solely because of the meaning of the terms it contains.

Time preference rate: the rate by which people prefer goods in the present to goods in the future. This rate principally determines the rate of interest.

Transaction: a purchase or sale of any commodity.

Transactions cost: the expenses that come about because a transaction takes place; e.g., bargaining cost.

Unemployment: a state of affairs in which a worker's services are not in demand at a given wage rate.

Utilitarianism: a system of ethics that maintains that the good is whatever maximizes happiness.

Utility: the value of a good to a consumer.

Value: the attribute of a good that fits for use, or enables it to secure other goods in exchange on the market.

Value, subjective theory of: the view, developed by the Austrian School, that economic value is not an inherent property of a good. Rather, it is determined by the preferences of those who wish to acquire the good.

Recommended Readings

Everyone who reads this book should also read Henry Hazlitt, *Economics in One Lesson* (Arlington House, 1979). It is a superb account of how economic theory applies to the real world.

You will also find extremely helpful Murray Rothbard's brilliant, and very short book *What Has Government Done to Our Money?* (Ludwig von Mises Institute, 1990). This is a very clear presentation of Austrian monetary theory. If you want to know how the current U.S. monetary system got started, the same author's *The Case Against the Fed* (Ludwig von Mises Institute, 1994) is a good place to begin.

The two greatest twentieth-century works of the Austrian School are Ludwig von Mises's, *Human Action* (Ludwig von Mises Institute, [1949] 1998) and Murray Rothbard's, *Man, Economy, and State* (Ludwig von Mises Institute, [1962] 1993). You will probably find them hard going, however, and you should be satisfied with reading whatever interests you in them. Rothbard is much easier than most parts of *Human Action*.

Probably the best way to get the flavor of Mises is to start with essays in his *Planning for Freedom* (Libertarian Press, 1980) and the essay "Planned Chaos" in *Socialism* (LibertyClassics, 1982).

About the Author

Dr. David Gordon is a Senior Fellow at the Ludwig von Mises Institute, and editor of *The Mises Review*. He was educated at UCLA, where he earned his PhD in intellectual history, and is the author of *Resurrecting Marx: The Analytical Marxists on Exploitation, Freedom and Justice; The Philosophical Origins of Austrian Economics*; and *Critics of Marx*. He is also editor of *Secession, State & Liberty*, and co-editor of H.B. Acton's *Morals of Markets and Other Essays*. Dr. Gordon is a contributor to such journals as *Analysis, The International Philosophic Quarterly, The Journal of Libertarian Studies*, and *The Quarterly Journal of Austrian Economics*.

INDEX

Action, 13, 17–31
    allocating means, 31
    alternative, 135–37
    axiom, xiii, 17–26, 37, 87–89, 95, 175
    complex choices, 30
    goal of, 23, 24, 29–30
    indifference objection, 43–46
    as means to achieve ends, 24, 26, 29–30
    preference, 26–33, 44, 46, 49–53, 59–68, 78, 88, 155
    propositions, derive, 87
    radically uncertain, 25
    ranking, cardinal and ordinal, 31, 44, 48, 51–53, 92–93
    voluntary, 52
Aristotle, 3
Austrian School, xii, 22, 39–40, 47, 88–92, 96–101, 133–34, 154, 175
    supposed, so-called "radical subjectivists," 50

Bentham, Jeremy, 28–29
Böhm-Bawerk, Eugen von, 96–101, 176
    Capital and Interest, 96
    Karl Marx and the Close of His System, 96
Buchanan, James, (Nobel laureate in economics), 88
Buridan's ass, 43, 45–46
Butler, Bishop Joseph, 4

Carlyle, Thomas, x
Choosing, 29, 43–44
Classical doctrine, 90

Clinton, Hillary, 5, 37
Cohen, Morris, 39
Common sense, 21
Communist governments, 90
Crusoe economics, 51
Curves
    demand and supply, 65–80, 87–88
    elastic and inelastic, 73–75
    intersection, 88
    shift, 79–81

Defoe, Daniel, 51

Economics
    science of, 17, 21
    "vulgar," 91
    why study, ix
Edgeworth boxes, 45
Engels, Friedrich, 91
Equality, 120–21
Ethics, 112–13, 124–25
Exchange, 51–53, 57–68, 91, 94–96, 134–42, 167
    "double coincidence of wants," 139
    indirect, 135–141
    transactions costs, 140–42

Goods (value)
    exchange and use, 95
    labor–hours, 91
    utility, 92

Gossen, Heinrich, 47
Government intervention, 109–15, 175
    ceiling prices, 109–11
    irrational goals, 115
    exchange rates, 170–73
    and labor unions, 128
    mandated benefits, 127
    and unemployment, 123
    minimum wages, 119–29
    rationing, 114
Gresham's Law, 172–73

Hayek, F.A.
    Law, Legislation & Liberty, 155
Hedonism, psychological, 27, 32
Historicists, xii
Hutchins, R.M., 20

Indifference curves, 45
Infinite regress, 24
Institutionalists, xii

Johnson, Paul
    Intellectuals, 91

Kautsky, Karl, 91
Keynes, John Maynard
    General Theory, 136
Kierkegaard, Søren, 29
King Enrique el Impotente of Castile, 27
Kirzner, Israel
    Opportunity, Perception, and Profit, 50

Labor theory of value, 91–101, 175
Labor unions, 128–29
    and coercion, 128
Law of demand, 23, 69
Law of supply, 71
Lenin, V.I., 91
Locke, John, 154, 176

Logic
    a priori reasoning, 163
    analogous proposition, 107–08
    argument, 2, 5
        categorical syllogism, 9, 86
        reductio, 106–08
    assumption, 171
    conclusion, 1, 5, 112–14, 135–36
    circular reasoning, 156
    deductive method, xii, 1–17, 37
    diagrammed, 2, 6
        intersect, 6
    hypothesis, 49
    inference
        correct, 2, 3
        rules, 2
    laws of, 3
        identity, 4
        non–contradiction, 4, 85–86, 106–07
        excluded middle, 4
    propositions, commonsense, 31
    premises 1, 112–14
        contingent, 12
        hypothetical, 10, 86, 88
        initial, 17
        intermediate, 12
        major, 2
        necessary proposition, 11–12
        stronger, 10, 25
        value judgment, 113, 171, 175–76
        weak, 63
    statement, 1, 172
    validity, 5–9, 66, 112–14

Marginal buyers and sellers, 108–09
Market interference, 105–06
Marx, Karl, 1, 90–101, 175
    Capital, volume I, 101
    scientific socialism, 90
Marxism, 91–101
    ABCs, 91–92
    basic mistake, 94–96
    circular reasoning, 98–100
    and efficient workers, 97
    final anomaly, 99–101
    important fallacy, 97–99

labor comparison in different goods, 98–99
not subjectivist, 94
and "socially necessary" labor, 98–99
Menger, Carl, xii, 154–55, 176
Principles of Economics, 154
Mill, John Stuart, 28–29
Minimum wage rule, 124–25
Mises, Ludwig von, xiii, 9, 17, 115–16, 125, 155–60, 176
Human Action, 69
The Theory of Money and Credit, 157
Molière, Jean-Baptiste Poquelin, ix
Money
aurephobia, 151
commodity, 165
convergence of goods used as, 144–49
demonetization, 173–74
fiat, 159, 175
gold standard, 164–74
medium of exchange, 143–46
origin, 154–58
properties of, 149–51, 164
purchasing power as estimate, 157, 163
regression theorem, 154–60, 164, 173
as store of value, 152–60
supply and demand, 155, 165
utility value as a good, 158
value gain, 144

New Deal, xi
Newton's first law of motion, 22
Nozick, Robert
"Coercion" in *Socratic Puzzles*, 52

Objective laws, 93
Observation,
underlying level of, 22
Okun, Arthur, 120

Petro, Sylvester
The Kohler Strike, 129
Philosophical
assumption, 119–21
doctrine, 89, 115

Policy analysis, 105–16
Praxeology, 47, 87–89, 95, 101, 145, 152
Price, 59–68
arbitrageurs, 64, 168–70
ceiling, 110
competition, 63
control, 105–16
equilibrium or market clearing, 77
expectation, 111, 124
as expressed preferences, 88–89
law of one, 64, 77
surpluses and shortages, 172
Psychological
behaviorism and subjectivism, 93
hypothesis, 29
state, 45, 48

Queen Isabella, 27

Rawls, John
"difference principle," 120
A Theory of Justice, 120
Renaissance, 90
Ricardo, David, 90, 137
Robertson, Sir Dennis, 88
Robbins, Lord Lionel, 32
Roosevelt, Franklin D., x
Rothbard, Murray, xiii, 43, 151, 173, 176
Ethics of Liberty, 115
Russell, Bertrand, 1

Salerno, Joseph, 151
Schedules, supply and demand, 65–68, 155
Schmoller, Gustav, xii
Schumpeter, Joseph, 48
History of Economic Analysis, 48
Shaw, George Bernard, 21
Sisyphus, 30
Smith, Adam, 90, 137
Social Security account, 127
Sombart, Werner, xii, 47
Subjective valuation, 33, 49–50, 81, 90–93

Tautology, 38–41
Tennyson, Alfred Lloyd, 168
Twentieth century, 90

Uncertain future, 24
Utilitarianism, 29
Utility
    comparisons, 92
    marginal, 26–28, 41–42, 46–48, 50–51, 60,
    65, 166
    not psychological law of "satiation of
    wants," 47
    ranking, 31–32
    relevant unit, 49, 60, 78

Veblen, Thorstein, xii

Wages
    demand schedule and, 124
    expectation, 124
    marginal buyer, 123
    minimum
        and false claims, 125
        and unemployment, 123
    as specific kind of labor, 121
    supply and demand, 122–24
    zone of indeterminacy, 126–27
World War II, 114

Notes

Notes

Notes

Notes

Notes

Notes

Notes

Notes

Notes

Notes

Notes

Notes

Notes

Notes